"Human services?... That must be so rewarding."

A PRACTICAL GUIDE FOR PROFESSIONAL DEVELOPMENT

"Human services?... That must be so rewarding."

by

Gail S. Bernstein, Ph.D.

Director, Adult Services
John F. Kennedy Child Development Center
Associate Professor, Preventive Medicine and Biometrics
Associate Professor, Psychiatry
University of Colorado School of Medicine
Denver

and

Judith A. Halaszyn

Assistant Residential Director
Jefferson County Community Center for Developmental Disabilities
Colorado

·P·A·U·L·H·
BROOKES
PUBLISHING CO.

Baltimore • London • Toronto • Sydney

Paul H. Brookes Publishing Co.
Post Office Box 10624
Baltimore, Maryland 21285-0624

Typeset by Brushwood Graphics Inc., Baltimore, Maryland.
Manufactured in the United States of America by
Thomson-Shore, Dexter, Michigan.

Illustrations by Jeff Slemons.

Library of Congress Cataloging-in-Publication Data
Bernstein, Gail S. 1947–
  "Human services? . . . That must be so rewarding."
  Bibliography: p.
  Includes index.
  1. Human services—Vocational guidance. 2. Human services person-
nel. I. Halaszyn, Judith A. II. Title.
HV10.5.B36 1989   361′.0023′73   88-19321
ISBN 1-55766-007-7

"She had never been especially impressed by the heroics of the people convinced they are about to change the world. She was more awed by the heroism of those who are willing to struggle to make one small difference after another."

Ellen Goodman
Close to Home

Contents

About the Authors

Gail S. Bernstein has had 10 years of experience providing human services and 10 years of experience as a consultant, teacher, and manager of human services professionals. She received her Ph.D. in 1978 (Studies in Behavioral Disabilities) from the University of Wisconsin. Dr. Bernstein is currently Director of Adult Services at the John F. Kennedy Child Development Center at the University of Colorado School of Medicine. She also holds the positions of Associate Professor, Preventive Medicine and Biometrics, and Associate Professor, Psychiatry, at the University of Colorado School of Medicine.

Judith A. Halaszyn received her B.A. from Loretto Heights College in Denver in 1984 and is currently Assistant Residential Director of the Jefferson County Community Center. She has had 23 years of experience providing and managing human services.

Introduction

The following chapters cover topics human services workers usually don't discuss. Most of us are trained, either in school or on the job, in methods of providing services. Our training seldom, if ever, includes consideration of these questions:

Why am I doing this?
What do I expect to get out of it?
What do I expect to accomplish?
What are or should be my values as I provide services?
How do I act while I provide services?
How do I manage the stressful aspects of working in human services?

This book is about those questions. The focus here, unlike most human services texts, is clearly on the provider of services rather than on the recipient. That focus is not from any lack of concern for the people who receive our services. Instead, it is the result of our conviction that the most effective and humane services are delivered by people who have clear answers to the questions listed above.

Chapter 1, **On Knowing Yourself,** addresses personal motives, goals, and limits for the human services worker. In Chapter 2, **On Minding Other People's Business,** we address client rights and the dignity of the individual. Chapter 3, **Human Problems, Human Services Values,** suggests fundamental values for the human services. Chapters 4, 5, 6, and 7 cover professional behavior, specifically professional relationships, time management, communication, and professional development. Chapter 8 is about the necessity for and ways to improve stress management. The closing chapter reflects on human services as a career, highlighting interviews with long-time professionals in the field.

The skills addressed here are complex and difficult to acquire. Each chapter is an introduction to a topic about which many books and scholarly articles have been written. We suggest you read and work through no more than a chapter a week, taking time to thoroughly consider the questions raised.

Our purpose is to provide a book that is, above all, practical and applied rather than academic. While there are references, no attempt was made to thoroughly examine the vast literature pertaining to the topics covered here. Instead, we relied on a few selected references, the generosity of our colleagues and students in sharing information, and our collective experience of over 40 years in human services.

Our audience consists of people who currently provide or will be providing human services. Our text is intended for: 1) students in undergraduate and community college programs who are entering practicum programs, and 2) people currently working in any of the human services. This includes at least current and future social workers, counselors, probation officers, direct care providers, child care and youth workers, mental health workers, therapists, developmental disabilities workers, case managers, rehabilitation personnel, geriatrics specialists, independent living center staff, psychologists, and advocates. As former teachers, we also think educators may find this book useful.

Sometimes professionals are defined as people who hold graduate degrees. One of us fits this definition, the other does not. We both reject it. Instead, we see professionalism as a function of how people behave on the job. Whenever "human services professionals" are referred to in this book, the intent is to include everyone providing human services, regardless of level or type of education.

Acknowledgments

Many of our friends and colleagues have contributed to this book. We owe thanks to John Leslie, Karen Litz, and Dr. Jon Ziarnik for specific content ideas; to Randy Chapman for several vignettes related to legal issues; to Mary Ervolina for several vignettes related to social work; to students in Human Services classes at Metropolitan State College, for telling us why they want to work in human services, and for our many conversations during our guest lectures for them.

Thanks are also extended to Brenda Watson and Dr. Bob Watson for their invitations to come into their classes, and to Brenda Watson for her comments on the manuscript; to the many people currently working in human services who were willing to tell us why they do it and to share stories about their work.

Thanks also to Becky Albracht, Therese Hustis, David Calderwood, Roger Freeby, Sara Johnson, and Guinn Rogers for working through and commenting on a draft version of the entire manuscript as we wrote it.

Nina Cruchon, Cami Learned, Sally Mather, and Megan Miller provided extensive editorial feedback and much-needed moral support during the entire writing process. Their comments led to innumerable improvements, and their encouragement kept us going. Dr. Andy Sweet and Dr. Jon Ziarnik read and commented on the last draft version of the manuscript and helped shape the final version with their thoughtful suggestions. Our artist, Jeff Slemons, turned our verbal descriptions into wonderful artwork that clearly captures the spirit of the book.

Finally, heartfelt thanks to everyone at Brookes Publishing, and especially to Melissa Behm, for taking a chance on something a little different, for considerable patience with missed deadlines, and for making us, as usual, such an integral part of the publishing process.

In memory of our fathers

Allen L. Bernstein, Ed.D.
I think he would have liked this book.
G.S.B.

Michael J. Halaszyn
He would have been so proud.
J.A.H.

"Human services?... That must be so rewarding."

SECTION I

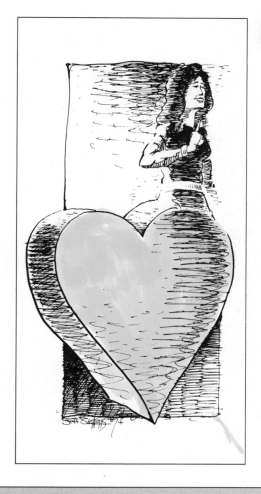

HUMAN
SERVICES
PROFESSIONAL

CHAPTER 1

ON KNOWING YOURSELF

OR

What's a Nice
Person Like You Doing in a Job Like This?

OBJECTIVES

To be able to:

1. Identify your motives, goals, and aspirations for selecting a human services career.
2. Identify personal characteristics that may limit your professional performance.
3. Identify typical limits on your performance that are due to external problems.

THE TALE OF DISILLUSIONED DIANA

One year after college graduation, four members of the class of '87 gather at Joe's Fern Bar to compare notes on their new careers and professions. In the group are an accountant, a lawyer, a computer analyst, and Diana, a probation officer. There is talk of opportunities to advance within organizations, and comparisons of office sizes and amenities. The bragging moves on to who has the most perks, the most trips coast to coast, and who has rubbed elbows with the movers and shakers. As the bravado gradually diminishes, someone turns to Diana and asks her about her work. Diana tries to evade the attention with pat phrases like: "I enjoy the challenge," "It's very demanding dealing with people," and "It gives me a sense of fulfillment."

Later, back in her downtown efficiency apartment, Diana lets the frustration and disillusionment from the reunion flood over her. Feeling cheated and frustrated with the fact that she receives no perks and no amenities, and has mountains of paperwork, no easy answers, and problems bigger than she has ever imagined, Diana wants a way out. She picks up the evening paper and begins to circle want ads while muttering to herself: "No one ever warned me what human services would really be like."

The doorbell rings in Diana's apartment. It is a package delivery. She starts to open the box and thinks: "Oh—it's the book I ordered last month. It's probably too late to be useful now, but I don't have anything better to do." She opens to page one of *"Human services? . . . That must be so rewarding."*

KNOWING YOUR PROFESSIONAL MOTIVATION

"If we do not care for ourselves, we cannot care for others."

(Gaylin, 1981, p. 34)

People who choose to work in one of the human services have chosen to serve other people, to "do good." Therefore, the obvious answer to the question of why you have selected human services work is therefore something like: "to help people." Having said that, you have identified your motives for doing human services work, right?

Well, not exactly. It is important to be more specific about your motives for engaging in a particular type of work. It is important to identify what makes you want to come to work every day and what rewards you get out of your work. If the work you do does not meet your professional needs, you are not likely to be able to do a good job of meeting other people's needs. Most of us need to do work that makes us feel good about ourselves: work that we see as valuable. This is especially necessary for human services professionals because we often get mixed messages from both our colleagues and the world at large about the worth of what we do.

THE "JUST A . . ." PROBLEM

If we do not value what we do, the "just a" problem arises. This problem is most obvious at parties when the answer to the question: "What do you do?" is: "Oh, I'm just a social worker," or: "Just a child care worker," or: "Just a direct care staff worker." People who describe their work by saying: "I'm just a . . ." are saying that what they do is not really valuable in their own eyes, or in the eyes of other people. It is the authors' contention that, if you are going to work in human services, you need to know what makes this work valuable to you, to the people you serve, and to society as a whole.

DEFINING MOTIVES: THE OUTSIDE VIEW

Let's go back to the party where, when asked what you do, you have identified yourself as a human services professional. If you have been chatting with someone who is not in human services, chances are the response will be something like: "That must be very challenging work," or: "I wish I could do that, but there's not enough money in it," or: "Oh, you must have so much patience," or, most often: "Oh, that must be so rewarding." What these comments really mean is: "I don't understand what you get out of doing that stuff, but I guess it's good someone wants to do it." Similarly, spouses, parents, and close friends may react with blunt comments such as: "Why don't you want to work with normal people"? or: "How are you going to support yourself on such a low salary"?

The issue reflected in these responses is that people in human services typically receive fewer tangible (especially financial) rewards than people working in business receive. People who find human services work satisfying are able to identify the nonmonetary rewards they get from their work, such as seeing a small but significant change in someone's life or being thanked by someone who has used their services.

DEFINING MOTIVES: SOME HUMAN SERVICES VIEWS

The authors interviewed a variety of human services professionals concerning their reasons for choosing to work in the field of human services. Students who were beginning studies in a college human services department were also interviewed. Below is a sampling of their responses:

A nurse in a rehabilitation facility:
   "I work with people because it's fun"!
Several direct service professionals:
   "It's different every day."
   "I'm able to make a real impact on someone's life."
   "I learn a lot: it's intellectually stimulating."
Three former teachers, now residential treatment supervisors:

"It's the difficult clients and their challenging problems that make it
worthwhile."

"I enjoy the people I work with."

"It's always changing."

A computer programmer who has done weekly volunteer work with
developmentally disabled adults for 6 years:

"It gives me a balance and puts everything in perspective."

Students in a human services program:

"It's a chance for me to give back to the system the help I have
received."

"A way to connect with the human race."

"It gives me a full heart to be able to help others."

Exercises

1-1.   Ask several human services professionals or human services students
       you know to list their motives for doing human services work.
1-2.   Write down the comments you have received from family and friends
       who do not understand your motives for choosing human services
       work.

THE TALE OF DISILLUSIONED DIANA, CONTINUED

Diana reads the first section, comes to the exercises, picks up a pencil
and begins writing answers as she says to herself: "It can't hurt, and
just maybe it will help me figure out what to do next. I really do enjoy
my job when I get a kid back in school and off the streets. It's also true
that I dread the long court hearings and destroyed parents when all
too often the kids get deeper into trouble with the law.

Mom would be delighted if I changed careers—became 're-
spectable' and not working with the 'dregs' as she calls them. Every
time she says that I get so angry . . .

Tomorrow I'll try to talk with Harry . . . he's been a probation officer for 10 years and still cares. I'll ask him how he keeps going."

IDENTIFYING YOUR OWN MOTIVES

It is important for you to know your motives for entering human services work. If you are not sure why you are doing the work you do, it
will be difficult to deal with the mixed social messages you will receive
about the worth of human services work.

This section of the chapter consists mostly of exercises designed to help you identify your motives for working in human services. Before the exercises start, however, consider the following rules of thumb for completing them:

1. It is okay to have selfish motives as well as unselfish ones. For instance, one motive shared by the authors for writing this book is to satisfy our need to help human services professionals. Another motive is to make some money from the sales of the book.
2. It is okay to have fun while you work. It is possible to do serious work and have a good time doing it. Do not feel there is something wrong with having fun at work.
3. It is also okay to have unselfish motives such as making people's lives a little easier.
4. It is *not* okay to do human services work because you think you *should* find it rewarding, or because you believe people will think you are a good person. Whatever you do, do it because *you* want to, not because someone else wants you to. People who genuinely like their work and find it rewarding usually do better work than people who do not like what they do.

Exercises

1-3. If you are still in training, you may not be familiar with what people in your profession do on a day-to-day basis. There are several ways to find out. Choose one of the following to do:
  a. Interview one or more people who are currently doing the type of work you plan to do. Ask them to describe what they do in the course of a typical day. Also, ask them to identify the tasks they find most satisfying and those they find least satisfying.
  b. By signing up for internships and/or volunteer work, expose yourself to a variety of experiences in the type of organizations and professions you are considering.
  c. Arrange to shadow someone in your profession for a day, noting the different things he or she does. If you do not know anyone to ask, call an agency, and explain who you are and why you want to shadow someone. Anticipate the fact that the person you shadow needs to get approval from a supervisor and may have trouble finding time on her or his calendar to fit you in.

During all these exercises, be sure to note not only core activities such as counseling, but also support activities such as paperwork and driving.

1-4. Using your experience, or the information you collected while doing exercise 1-3, write a description of a typical workday for the type of job that interests you. Following is an example:

    8:00 Report in, check with secretary for messages, return phone calls from people seeking benefits.

    9:00 Conduct meetings with potential benefits recipients, complete multiple forms for each person.

  11:00 Compile memos to files for people seen today; send paperwork and recommendations to supervisor.

  12:00 Lunch

  12:30 Attend department meeting.

   1:30 Investigate possible child abuse situation; make on-site assessment (includes 45 minutes travel round trip).

   3:30 Meet with department attorney to discuss findings.

   4:00 Finish memos to files.

   4:30 Make list of things to do for tomorrow.

   4:45 Leave, get stuck in rush hour traffic.

   5:30 Arrive home hot, fussy, and frustrated.

1-5. Using all the information you have gathered about your chosen career, answer the following questions:

    a. What am I or will I be required to do that I like to do?

    b. Of my answers to a., which do I like to do more than any of the other activities? Why?

    c. What am I or will I be required to do that I do not like to do?

    d. Of my answers to c., which am I most likely to avoid? Why?

Knowing Your Limits

"Reform yourself as well as the world."

(Weldon, 1984, p. 88)

*"We think that ethical practice requires that counselors determine *with whom* and *in what circumstances* they are unable to be effective and that they then make an appropriate referral."*

(Corey, Corey, & Callanan, 1988, p. 323)

The previous section of this chapter was devoted to helping you identify what you get out of doing human services work. This section is about identifying limits that interfere with your performance. Why is it important for you to do something many people find unappealing? It is important to know your limits because no one is perfect, and no one has all the answers. While in the future you may have some of the answers that you do not have now, you will also have other questions that have not occurred to you yet. In the long run, you will be more effective if you assume the following:

1. I do not have all the answers and probably do not even know all the important questions.
2. Therefore, I am going to make mistakes.
3. It is okay to make mistakes.
4. It is *not* okay to make the same mistakes over and over.
5. It is not only okay, but also desirable, that I ask for help when I do not know what to do.

Personal Limits

Each of us has a different, unique combination of strengths and limitations. There are, however, some common problems people in human services often encounter:

You Do Not Love (or Sometimes Even Like) Everyone You Are Supposed to Serve   This is a tough lesson to learn, particularly when you have just started working in human services. However, there are few saints among us. It is perfectly normal (if not always nice) to have personal likes and dislikes. So, most of us have to learn that we like some of the people we serve more than others, and we also like some of our colleagues more than others. This is acceptable, as long as you know how you feel and work on behaving professionally toward everyone, not just those you like. It is not only possible, but necessary, to treat your colleagues and the consumers of your services with respect and courtesy, regardless of how you feel about them.

Further, not all the people you serve will like you. Some will resent what you seem to represent (e.g., privilege, government control), others will resent needing help from anyone, and some will resent your "professional expertise."

You Will Not Be Able to Save Everyone   You are not going to achieve the outcome you prefer with everyone you serve. Sometimes this occurs because, first, you need better skills. For instance, if your work with foster families results in an encounter with someone who has a drinking problem, you may not know how to help. The second reason you may not achieve the desired outcome is that some people do not want to be helped in the way you want to help them. For example, you may be trying to help a family keep a severely disturbed child at home, but the family may want you to find an out-of-home placement. The third reason is that sometimes people do not want the same outcomes you want for them. For example, a couple may want to save their marriage even though you feel doing so is unhealthy for both of them. A fourth reason is that sometimes you simply do not have enough control over the situation to achieve the desired outcome. One example is the person receiving counseling who shops for a physician who will prescribe psychotropic medications, no matter how unnecessary. Human services professionals often have to decide whether any good is likely to come from a human services intervention.

There Is Never Enough Time This is related to the problem of not being able to save everyone. There is nearly always more to do and more people who might be served than there is time to serve them. Human services professionals who do not learn to live with this lesson generally burn out rather quickly. You have to learn to manage professional time (see Chapter 5) and to take time to meet your nonprofessional needs. Most of us have relationships with friends, partners, or children and activities (e.g., in areas of recreation, hobbies, and community service) that are important to us and are not work related. If we fail to meet our nonprofessional needs, our professional performance usually suffers.

There Will Always Be Things about Your Work and the People You Work with that Cause a Strong Emotional Reaction In situations such as this, something "pushes your buttons." You do not react rationally, even though you know you are overreacting. It may be a certain tone of voice, a specific type of problem, or a form to fill out. All of us have button pushers. The first step toward coping with things that set you off is to figure out what they are. For instance, you may have a colleague who's voice sounds just enough like your mother that you react to her as if she were your mother instead of a peer.

You May Not Want to Do Human Services Work for the Rest of Your Life Many people have more than one career during their lives: human services professionals are no exception. One common reason for a career change is development of new interests, either in a different aspect of human services or in something altogether different. Another common reason for a career change is that you no longer find your work rewarding enough. There is nothing wrong with this. Seldom do we find the same things rewarding throughout our lives.

External Limits

The limits described in the previous section are personal limits: you may not like everyone, you cannot help everyone, you do not have enough time. There is another type of limit also encountered by human services workers, specifically, the limits inherent in the construction of our systems for delivering human services. There are so many examples of external, systemic limits that we will only mention a few.

There Is Not Enough Money There are two main financial limits in human services; the type of limit depends on whether or not a particular service is an *entitlement* program. Entitlement programs must by law serve everyone who meets the basic eligibility criteria for them. Public schools, for example, are entitlement programs: they must serve all children of school age. When entitlement programs do not have enough money, everyone is served but not as well as they would be served with additional resources. When a human services program is not an entitlement program, what usually occurs is that there is not enough money to serve all eligible persons.

Some Programs Work Against Social Values Instead of Promoting Them American society claims to want to keep families together, but the current human services system sometimes works against families. Consider, for example, families with children who have severe physical and cognitive disabilities. Some social services systems provide the special services needed to support severely disabled children only if the children move to foster homes or to institutions. Another example of systems working against social values can be found in rehabilitation programs. The stated purpose of most of these programs is to get the people they serve to the point where rehabilitation services are no longer needed. However, when a person is successfully rehabilitated, the agency is punished by losing the funds that were used for serving that person; these are fees the agency needs to survive.

Also, there are welfare programs that do not pay benefits for children to women whose husbands live at home. The result is that some couples in need of money to care for their children have to separate in order to get the money. These examples illustrate the fact that American society has just begun to identify some of the systems changes needed to support social values instead of fighting them.

No One Knows Enough There are some human problems no one knows enough about to solve completely. Human services professionals do not have the knowledge, for example, to cure all alcoholics or all child molesters.

Systemic limits can ultimately be overcome only by people with the power and knowledge to change them. If you want to devote yourself to changing systemic limits in human services, you will need to become an advocate, an administrator, a policymaker, or a researcher.

Exercises

1-6. List all of the personal limits that can potentially interfere with your professional performance. Pick the three that could cause the most interference.

Examples: Unreliable car, job requires lots of local travel
New in town, not familiar with local resources
Mother was an alcoholic, and anger at her will probably
interfere with ability to help other substance abusers

1-7.   List your personal strengths that compensate for the limits you listed
above.
Examples: Thoroughly familiar with public transportation
Good at doing practical research, finding out about local
resources
Have been a recipient of social services and know how it
feels

1-8.   List all of the external limits that are likely to interfere with your professional performance. Pick the three most serious in relation to your current or anticipated responsibilities. Some common examples include:

overcrowded office space	noisy work areas
insufficient staff	limited funding
waiting lists for services	federal regulations
unrealistic deadlines	bureaucracy

1-9.   Of the limits you listed in answer to 1-8, which are most likely to bother
you? Why? You may find it useful to discuss these exercises with your
classmates or colleagues. (You are not the only one with limits!)

Which Way Do the Scales Tip?

"TANSTAAFL
There ain't no such thing as a free lunch.**"**

(Heinlein, 1968, p. 129)

No matter what type of work you choose to do, it will have some advantages and some disadvantages. Some of what you do will give you
the professional rewards you desire, and some of what you do will be
unpleasant to you (this is true in most jobs). Each of us is unique in
terms of what we find rewarding and what we find unpleasant. Further,
each of us is different in our judgment of what unpleasant activities we
are willing to engage in, and how much, in order to do the things we
find professionally rewarding. Each of us is different in the level of professional reward we need to keep doing what we do.

The point of all this is that it is not enough to know what your
professional rewards and costs are. You also need to know what sort of
balance you require between reward and cost for the end result to be
positive. Most of us can tell whether or not we are happy with our
work. When we are happy with our work, we like going to work in the
morning and we feel proud of what we do. When we are not happy with
our work, we usually do not jump out of bed bright-eyed and bushy-

tailed. (Some of us, of course, never jump out of bed bright-eyed and bushy-tailed, but that's a different problem.)

The difficult part is usually not the task of figuring out whether or not you are happy with your work. Instead, the difficulty lies with identifying the specific factors that make the difference between being happy professionally and wanting to find a different job or even a different profession. People can be dissatisfied with their work for any one of a number of reasons. They may be spending too much time doing things they find unpleasant. They may be doing too few of the things they find rewarding. Or, the problem may be both too few rewards and too many "punishers."

To complicate matters even further, sometimes people working in human services are dissatisfied not because they dislike their work, but because of the effects their work has on their personal lives. Most human services professionals cannot help spending some of their nonwork time thinking about and often worrying about the people they serve. *When you work in human services, you can't punch out!* We take worries about the people we serve home with us, and usually find it very difficult to simply shut a file drawer and forget them at 5:00 P.M. However, if your work takes too much of your attention during the rest of your life, you may find yourself dissatisfied with that work. It may have a negative effect on your personal life, particularly your personal relationships. That is why it is important to find a balance between worklife and homelife. In Chapters 5 and 8 we discuss ways to manage time and stress so that this is possible.

Exercises

1-10. On the *Advantages* side of the chart shown below, list all the rewards you get from your work. Or, if you are a student, list the rewards you expect to get. On the *opposite* side, list all the disadvantages you get or expect to get from your work.

Advantages   Disadvantages

Do the advantages outweigh the disadvantages? You may want to repeat this exercise every 3 or 6 months.

THE TALE OF DISILLUSIONED DIANA CONTINUES

Two weeks later, Diana thinks: "Finally, a quiet evening, no home visits to do, nothing good on the tube. Maybe I'll work on those exercises again. It sure helped to talk with Harry. In fact, I've been feeling more positive about my job lately. I guess mostly I worry that I'm not skilled enough to solve the problems my clients have, and I'm afraid I'll let them down.

" Well, let's see what my answers to Exercise 1-10 look like."

Disadvantages

High recidivism rate with juvenile offenders
Red tape and more red tape
Office in a dangerous part of town
No respect from family and some of my friends
Clients and families resent me (no, they resent what I stand for: courts, criminal records, failure)

Advantages

Experiencing the satisfaction of seeing a kid "make it"
Having a family and a client say "thanks"
My supervisor encourages me to attend seminars and workshops to improve my skills
Co-worker support
My hours are very flexible
I have the authority to make decisions and to be responsible for them

"Hmm—it's about even. Somehow, putting it on paper makes it real. I think I'll hang it on the wall by my desk as a reminder, and add to both lists as I think of things."

CHAPTER 2

ON MINDING
OTHER PEOPLE'S BUSINESS

OR

Who Appointed You?

OBJECTIVES

To be able to:

1. Be sensitive to the humanity of people receiving human services.
2. Be aware of the rights of people who receive human services, and of the implications of those rights for service providers.

Put yourself into the following story: Mr. Nosey Neighbor, who has an answer to every problem from split ends to toxic waste, stops you as you leave for work in the morning. "Say, I see you have leaves plugging up your gutters. Now, the way to fix that is (blah, blah, blah). We have to keep up property values in the neighborhood (blah, blah, blah)." This is the last thing you want to hear at 7:30 in the morning as you leave for work. You feel yourself getting angrier and angrier and as you get into your car, you mutter: "Who appointed you as my watchdog, anyway"?

" Can we do good to others, but on their terms?"

(Rothman, 1981, p. 95)

People First

Everyone in human services works, directly or indirectly, to help people. In fact, a desire to help people is the reason most of us choose human services work in the first place. Unfortunately, we sometimes forget that people are the center of our efforts. When we focus on the

15

problem instead of the person, we lose touch with the desire to help *people* and we lose effectiveness. It is important to remember that the people we serve are people first and clients second.

One of the most serious mistakes any human services worker can make is to focus on and emphasize only the problems of the people she or he is trying to serve. We tend to devalue people when we see only their problems, faults, and lack of skills. We are all imperfect and we all have problems. Nonetheless, most of us manage to lead reasonably productive lives and to make some contribution to our world. We are all entitled to respect and recognition for our contributions. Perhaps one of the best known examples of a person who made a valuable contribution to the world but who had a difficult personal life was Eleanor Roosevelt. It is now common knowledge that her marriage was less than ideal, at least in its later years. And yet, she made one of the most enduring contributions to world peace of anyone in the twentieth century.

> "She didn't have a well-adjusted personality. She
> had character. Her work was not just thwarted love
> projected onto the world. It was a life lived on principle."
>
> (Goodman, 1985, pp. 60–61)

THE RIGHT TO BE TAKEN SERIOUSLY

> "Lashley also reported no apparent change in the general
> behavior of a rat when significant fractions—say, 10 per
> cent—of its brain were removed. But no one asked the rat
> its opinion."
>
> (Sagan, 1977, p. 30)

Who are the people in your life that *you* take seriously? Are the people you serve on this list? Here are some of the cues society uses to tell us which people to take seriously:

They carry briefcases
They wear three-piece suits
They have money
They have the keys
They have political power

When we take someone seriously, we:

Ask for their input

Listen to their opinions and suggestions

Address them in the same way we expect to be addressed (both using first names or both using last names)

Look at them and make eye contact when we talk with them

Assume what they want may be different from what we want for them

Interact with them in language they understand

Respect their physical space

When we do not take people seriously, we:

Do not give them our complete attention, often writing or talking on the phone while they are with us

Do not make eye contact with them

Assume we have the answers for them

Talk about the person in front of other people (often while he or she is standing there)

Do not ask for their input or suggestions

Address them by their first names and expect them to call us Ms., Mr., or Dr.

Invade their physical space without their permission

Interrupt or finish thoughts for them

It is important to take people seriously, especially the people you serve. If you do not take people seriously, you deny their worth as individuals. You also fail to gain their respect or trust, and therefore, you are not being effective.

Exercises

2-1. Describe at least two individuals you know who get taken seriously. How do people act around them?

2-2. Next, describe at least two individuals you know who do not get taken seriously. How do people act around them?

2-3. What differences between the two groups of people you described above stand out for you?

2-4. Describe in detail an experience you had in which you were not being taken seriously.

2-5. How did the experience you have just described make you feel?

2-6. Review the list of cues that reveal whom one should take seriously. What would you add? List 5 more cues that you use to tell you whom to take seriously.

2-7. Repeat Exercise 2-1 for things that tell you whom not to take seriously.

Fitting the Solution to the Problem

> "When all you have is a
> hammer, everything looks like a nail."
>
> Anonymous

Most of us in human services are trained to effectively use one particular type of approach to solving human problems. Counselors learn to counsel, therapists learn a particular type of therapy, and advocates learn to advocate and use legal solutions. It is natural to want to do what we are good at doing. However, there is a common pitfall that is easy to fall into: defining problems in ways that allow us to pick our favorite solution for them. Here is a classic example.

Several years ago, the first author was consulted about using a behavioral intervention to help a young woman with mental retardation to improve her communication skills. This seemed at first like a reasonable request. The people making the request were fairly skilled in teaching individuals like the young woman in question, and the consultant is an expert in behavioral interventions. The young woman's problem was that she almost always held her hand over her mouth while talking with people. During the discussion about this problem, the human services workers who made the referral were asked if the young woman in question was taking any medication (a standard question, because many medications affect how people act). The staff replied that she was taking female hormone supplements because she had a complete hysterectomy and could not produce any of those hormones on her own. Further discussion revealed that the way the young woman held her hand over her mouth allowed her to cover the moustache she had grown. Also, the hormone dosage had not been reviewed by a physician for some time. Finally, conversation with the young woman revealed that she was quite embarrassed by her facial hair. The consultant (the author) refused to recommend a behavioral intervention. Instead, a medical evaluation of hormone levels was recommended because improper levels of hormones in women can lead to the growth of male secondary sex characteristics such as facial hair.

The situation described above is a classic example of two typical traps for people in human services. First, no one asked the person receiving help what she thought was the problem. Second, the people working with her tried to apply the solution they were good at applying instead of applying the most effective solution for the problem.

The Least Intrusive Solution

"Sin No. 9: Poking hungrily, unasked, into someone's psyche.
(It is better to accept the facade, for most of us go to great
trouble building and maintaining one)"

(Bracken, 1969, p. 74)

"When human beings are playing for stakes of happiness
and self-knowledge, the only believable victories are
probably the temporary and partial ones."

(Mallon, 1984, p. 83)

It is almost always easier to identify other people's problems than our own. It is also easier to design solutions for others' problems than for our own. This leads to the temptation to offer considerably more assistance than is wanted or needed. Here is an example:

A young woman who is 17 years old, has a minimum wage job, and is pregnant goes to a human services agency. She asks if there are any classes she can attend that will teach her about nutrition for the child she is going to have. The counselor suggests a class that is located an hour's bus ride away and costs $50.00. In addition, the counselor recommends enrollment in a vocational school, so that the young woman can get a better job, and assertiveness training, because she appears to be rather shy. The young woman shakes her head and leaves. The counselor does not understand why the woman left.

The counselor goes home at the end of the day, decides not to go to exercise class because it is too much trouble, and proceeds directly to his lawyer's office. There he discusses his divorce settlement.

How many of us always have sparkling clean homes, perfectly balanced budgets, completely nutritious diets, totally fulfilling personal relationships, and satisfying, successful careers? It is hardly fair to try to restructure someone else's life if your own is not in order. We cannot expect the people we serve to be more sane, more well-adjusted, more honest, or more independent than we ourselves. Most of us cope as best we can with the trials and tribulations of being human, winning temporary victories and suffering occasional setbacks. People do have problems that can be solved with outside assistance; that is why human services exist. However, not every problem requires a human services intervention, nor does everyone with a problem want such assistance. Further, most people who do accept our assistance want it to be as unintrusive as possible.

How can we determine whether the solutions we propose as human services professionals are as unintrusive as possible? Let us consider what we mean when we call a solution "intrusive." The more intrusive a solution is, the more it is:

Costly, in terms of time and/or money
Difficult to get transportation to
Disruptive to the person's privacy
Incompatible with the client's personal values, cultural or ethnic practices, and/or religious beliefs

Thus, for each problem we try to solve, we should ask whether the solution we select is, of all possible solutions to the problem, the least costly, the least disruptive, the easiest to get to, and the most compatible with client values.

Consider what the least intrusive solution might be for the situation cited earlier, in which the 17-year-old woman was looking for nutrition training for her new baby. Perhaps you could call the visiting nurses' office and arrange for the woman to call them at her convenience to arrange a time for a visit to her home. Or, you might check to find out whether the community school nearest her home offers a useful course. Both these alternatives are relatively inexpensive, are easy to use, and are not very disruptive to schedule.

Consumer Rights

> "Where should the authority of the caretaker
> leave off and the rights of the cared for begin?"
>
> (Rothman, 1981, pp. xi–xii)

The attitude of the American legal system toward the rights of people receiving services has undergone a significant change in the last 25 years. In the past, the courts assumed that human services professionals always acted in the best interests of the people they served, and those professionals were given boundless power. Currently, human service professionals are regarded very differently. This part of the chapter discusses the shift in underlying social assumptions that accompanied or caused the recent changes in judicial decisions about the law and human services.

The American government relies on a balance of powers. The authors of the United States Constitution wished to prevent a situation that permitted any one person or institution to possess too much power. Consequently, they designed a government that spread power over three branches. Furthermore, in the first ten amendments of the U.S. Constitution, collectively known as the Bill of Rights, certain rights are guaranteed to all citizens. These are:

Amendment I.   Congress shall make no law respecting an establishment of religion, or prohibiting the free exercise thereof; or abridging the freedom of speech, or of the press; or the right of the people peaceably to assemble, and to petition the Government for a redress of grievances.

Amendment II.   A well-regulated militia, being necessary to the security of a free State, the right of the people to keep and bear arms, shall not be infringed.

Amendment III.   No soldier shall, in time of peace be quartered in any house, without the consent of the owner, nor in time of war, but in a manner to be prescribed by law.

Amendment IV.   The right of the people to be secure in their persons, houses, papers, and effects, against unreasonable searches and seizures, shall not be violated, and no warrants shall issue, but upon probable cause, supported by oath or affirmation, and particularly describing the place to be searched, and the persons or things to be seized.

Amendment V.   No person shall be held to answer for a capital, or otherwise infamous crime, unless on a presentment or indictment of a Grand Jury, except in cases arising in the land or naval forces, or in the militia, when in actual service in time of war or public danger; nor shall any person be subject for the same offense to be twice put in jeopardy of life or limb; nor shall be compelled in any criminal case to be a witness against himself, nor be deprived of life, liberty, or property, without due process of law; nor shall private property be taken for public use without just compensation.

Amendment VI.   In all criminal prosecutions, the accused shall enjoy the right to a speedy and public trial, by an impartial jury of the State and district wherein the crime shall have been committed, which district shall have been previously ascertained by law, and to be informed of the nature and cause of the accusation; to be confronted with the witnesses against him; to have compulsory process for obtaining witnesses in his favor, and to have the assistance of counsel for his defense.

Amendment VII.   In suits at common law, where the value in controversy shall exceed twenty dollars, the right of trial by jury shall be preserved, and no fact tried by a jury shall be otherwise re-examined in any court of the United States, than according to the rules of the common law.

Amendment VIII.   Excessive bail shall not be required, nor excessive fines imposed, nor cruel and unusual punishments inflicted.

Amendment IX.   The enumeration in the Constitution, of certain rights, shall not be construed to deny or disparage others retained by the people.

Amendment X.   The powers not delegated to the United States by the Constitution, nor prohibited by it to the States, are reserved to the States respectively, or to the people.

You have undoubtedly studied the Bill of Rights in history, political science, and civics classes. What you may not know is that people receiving a variety of human services have often not had the same rights as the typical U.S. citizen. In fact,

> Violations of individual rights that would have created an instantaneous political and legal clamor had they been perpetrated by the police went unrecognized when they were perpetrated by social service professionals.

> (Glasser, 1981, p. 112)

One major example of a violation of individual rights takes place when there is lack of access to due process. Until very recently, a person with mental retardation or a mental illness could be locked up for treatment and automatically refused access to visitors, telephones, and attorneys. There were no procedures for determining whether these restrictions were necessary for treatment. The reason this was possible is that everyone assumed human services professionals always acted in the best interests of the people they served. Thus, these professionals were given unlimited power over the lives of the people receiving their assistance.

The courts no longer assume that human services workers are always benevolent (Glasser, 1981). Instead, the courts often appear to assume there is a conflict between the interests of service recipients and the interests of the providers of those services (Rothman, 1981). This assumption may be hard for some human services professionals to understand. After all, these professionals enter the field of human services to help people. Why should anyone assume they are enemies rather than friends? Following are three situations wherein human services workers did not appear to be acting in the client's best interest. These situations are based on actual cases.

In one instance, a vocational counselor worked with a young man to develop a plan for getting him a job. After the plan had been written, the man changed his mind about the type of work he wanted to do. The counselor was very upset with this change. Why? Because it meant redoing the required paperwork and thus meant more work for the counselor.

In a second situation, a married couple was participating in a special apartment program that provided support services for people with mental illnesses. One of the individuals started having problems that were best helped with more intensive support than the apartment program typically provided. The solution offered by the program was unsatisfactory: the couple was counseled to separate so that the person having problems could move to a more intensive service program.

The third situation involves a mismatch of job tasks and physical needs. Imagine spending your days sorting and boxing fish hooks. This is something one might do for the money, if nothing else was available, but one would be unlikely to choose this as a lifelong occupation. Even further: imagine having cerebral palsy and being severely impaired so that one is confined to a wheelchair, and can communicate only by typing very slowly on a communication board. Additionally, imagine having very limited motor control. This unfortunate situation occurred when a young man with severe physical disabilities was placed in a sheltered workshop packaging fish hooks because that was the only available job in the workshop.

In the first example, the counselor was more concerned with the demands on her time than with her client's wishes. In the second example, the service program was willing to break up a marriage rather than adjust the manner of service delivery. In the third example, the agency used the job that was available, rather than devising one that would be suited to the man's physical limitations. Each person was therefore put in a situation guaranteed to be frustrating and dehumanizing. No wonder the courts do not assume human services professionals always act in the best interests of the people they serve!

Ira Glasser, while serving as Executive Director of the American Civil Liberties Union, proposed three principles for permitting social programs to function while limiting unintended negative consequences:

1. The Bill of Rights applies to the human services and limits the powers of those services over the lives of the people being served (adapted from Glasser, 1981, p. 127). For example, no one can have his or her rights abridged without due process of law.

2. "Enforcement of constitutional limits is not self-executing and therefore requires an external force" (Glasser, 1981, p. 136). Glasser's statement implies the need for outside advocates who help protect the rights of people receiving services.
3. "Every program designed to help the dependent ought to be evaluated, not on the basis of the good it might do, but rather on the basis of the harm it might do. Those programs ought to be adopted that seem to be the least likely to make things worse" (Glasser, 1981, p. 145).

These principles may seem harsh to you in your role as a professional member of the human services field. Consider them when you respond to the exercise below. Then, decide if the principles still seem unreasonable.

HOW WOULD YOU WANT TO BE TREATED?

> "It is apparently natural behavior to treat the sick, the disabled, and the bereaved with curiosity and distaste, but it is also highly uncivilized."
>
> (Martin, 1985, p. 13)

People with physical disabilities sometimes refer to nondisabled people as being "temporarily able-bodied." This is a difficult concept for many of us to face, because no one likes the idea that one may not be able to do things one does now. However, of all the reasons one may someday need to receive human services, disability due to injury is surely one of the most common.

Suppose that one evening, while returning home from a friend's house where you attended a dinner party, your car is hit by another car driven by someone who has had too much to drink. You wake up to find yourself in the hospital, having permanently lost the use of your legs.

Exercises

2-8. Given the situation described above, do the research necessary to answer the following questions:
   a. What are your needs in all areas of life functioning?
   b. What resources in your community are available to help you meet those needs?
   c. Who will help you?
   d. How do you want to be treated?

e. How would this injury affect your current personal and professional goals?

MORE TALES OF DISILLUSIONED DIANA

As Diana reads Exercise 2-8, she shakes her head. "That nearly happened to me, although the injury wasn't permanent. Last summer, I tripped while jogging and really tore up my knee and leg. I was in a cast for months, first with a wheelchair and then on crutches. People were very different to me. They acted like my brain was in my knee, talked to me in simple words, offered—no, insisted—on assisting me and usually made things worse.

I quickly found out about limitations—like heavy doors to rest rooms that I couldn't pull with crutches. I was lucky I had a roommate then who could help me at home. Grocery shopping was a nightmare with kids crashing into me and people getting impatient and pushing past me. I nearly wiped out in the produce section because there was water on the floor and it was slippery.

That experience sure gave me a feel for this exercise. Now, let's see about the rest of the questions."

HUMAN

SERVICES

PROFESSIONAL

CHAPTER 3

HUMAN PROBLEMS, HUMAN SERVICES VALUES

OR

How Shall We Help?

OBJECTIVES

To be able to:

1. Acknowledge that human problems have complex, multiple causes.
2. Identify and avoid the pitfalls of blaming the victim and of acting morally superior.
3. Determine how a particular service relates to the four values described in the chapter.
4. Identify how cultural and ethnic differences can affect the delivery of human services.
5. Acknowledge the possibility that you may disagree with current social policy as practiced by your agency.

Mary is on welfare. Mary is a single mother with three children under the age of 5. Her only income is Aid to Families with Dependent Children (AFDC). She tried to work full-time, but she could not make enough money to pay for her child care and other bills. She is very depressed. One may ask: does Mary have a problem? If so, what is it? What solution would you recommend? How would you implement this solution?

The way in which human services professionals go about solving social problems depends in part on their values and assumptions. Usually, workers have assumptions about the causes of social problems, and opinions about how to design solutions for them. This chapter describes some of the ways values and assumptions can affect the work of the human services professional.

Causes of Social Problems

> "I understand that in the world there are people who are nuts. But I am also sure that the world can make people nuts."
>
> (Goodman, 1981, p. 22)

American society engages in an ongoing discussion about what social problems exist and how they should be solved. In fact, a large part of the American political process is devoted to this discussion. However, there is rarely, if ever, total agreement among government agencies about the nature, causes, and desirable solutions for these social problems. Consider, for example, a variety of typical reactions to Mary's story:

She needs affordable child care so that she can work
She needs to stop sleeping around and having children
She needs antidepressant medication
She needs to try harder
She needs psychotherapy
She needs a better job
She needs increased AFDC benefits
She needs child support payments from her children's father
She needs a society with values that make it acceptable and perhaps desirable for mothers of young children to receive government support to stay at home
She needs to use an effective means of birth control

Each of these solutions is based on a different assumption about the causes and solutions to Mary's problem. We live in a culture that emphasizes the individual. Individuals are expected to "pull themselves up by their boot straps" and improve their lot in life. On one hand, there is a self-reliant attitude: many people whose lots in life have improved significantly have the attitude that "I did it, and so can they, if they want to." On the other hand, there is the expectation of helping others. Our culture emphasizes helping the "less fortunate," an attitude that suggests some people are simply unlucky and therefore have less than the rest of us: less money, less support, less education, and so on.

The reality of our social problems is more complex than is evident in any one simple slogan. Human services professionals recognize that how a person acts at any given time is a function of four variables: the person's biological make-up, the person's current biological state, the person's history (e.g., education, upbringing, cultural background), and the person's current environment. The importance of each of these factors in the creation of a particular social problem varies from problem to problem. Examples of such variability may be found in cases of early infantile autism and in instances of child abuse.

Early Infantile Autism   Incidence of early infantile autism used to be attributed to indifferent treatment from cold mothers. However, research does not support this hypothesis. Instead, a strong biological relationship between organic damage and autism has been established (Romanczyk & Kistner, 1982). Good treatment and support can help control the effects of the autism so that persons with autism can live successfully in their communities (Lovaas, 1987), but there is no cure. The biological make-up of the autistic individual, rather than parental relationship, is very likely the major cause of the problem.

Child Abuse   There are a host of variables determining whether or not a child will be abused; the most important variables to examine are the parents' history and the child's current environment. Personal characteristics that place a parent at risk for abusing a child include: emotional disturbance, limited coping and problem-solving skills (especially when angry), low self-esteem, alcoholism, a history of having been an abused or neglected child, being a stepparent, and lack of emotional attachment to the child. In addition to certain personality characteristics, deficient parental resources are also risk factors. Deficient resources include: low socioeconomic status, being a single parent, having a large number of children, having children close together in age, having a lack of social supports, and having a lack of social and parenting skills. Finally, the question remains as to why only *some* parents with these characteristics abuse or neglect their children. One possible answer is that they become trapped in negative interactions that cycle them ever closer to abusive behavior (Burgess & Richardson, 1984).

The different causes of these two social problems should lead to different approaches to their solutions. On the one hand, the long-term solution to autism is likely to be found by scientists researching the organic causes of autism. In the meantime, of course, we will need to provide services for people with autism that help them to lead happier, more productive lives. The long-term solution to child abuse, on the other hand, is not likely to be found in a laboratory filled with test tubes and equipment. Instead, the solution probably lies with how we teach people to parent, and with the type of support society gives parents.

It is important for human services workers to be knowledgeable about the causes of the social problems they work on. This is the only way long-term solutions for these problems can be designed. It is also the only way the two common pitfalls of blaming the victim and of acting morally superior, can be avoided.

Exercises

3-1. Pick two social problems currently being addressed by one of the human services (examples of social problems might include teen pregnancy, child abuse, or care of the elderly). For each problem:
   a. Ask a sampling of people from a variety of professions what they think causes the problem.
   b. Ask the same people to describe how to solve the problems.
   c. Look at some of the current professional literature on causes of the problem and recommended solutions.
   d. Describe the similarities and differences between the answers you obtained for a., and b., and those you obtained for c.
   e. Do the solutions people recommend differ depending on what they say causes a problem?

PITFALLS

All of us who work in human services need to remain constantly aware of the complex causes of human problems, of new research findings on those causes, and of our attitudes toward people with problems. Additionally, we need to avoid what is probably the most common and most counterproductive pitfall in the field, specifically, that of *blaming the victim*. Blaming the victim involves suggesting a person is responsible for causing her or his problem. For instance, women whose husbands abuse them may be accused of doing something to deserve the abuse. Blaming the victim is a terrible thing to do for several reasons. Often the implied assumption is: "You're responsible for the problem, so go fix it." Also, blaming people for causing their own problems can make them feel worse about themselves ("I'm so awful, I got myself into this mess"). Lowered self-esteem is not likely to result in more effective problem solving.

> *"Sin No. 98: Acting morally superior toward someone busily sinning in some fashion that doesn't happen to tempt you or that you haven't been caught at yet."*
>
> (Bracken, 1969, p. 138)

Another pitfall for professionals in the human services is the temptation *to feel and act morally superior* to the people one is supposed to serve because one does not have their problem.

If it is hard for you to imagine falling into this trap, consider some typical reactions to smoking. People who have never smoked often cannot understand what anyone could possibly get out of that smelly habit, and behave as if smokers may not have the right to exist at all. Ex-smokers can easily start feeling morally superior, and can manifest the "I did it, why can't you" attitude. Smokers often swear that when they quit they will never be as self-righteous as some of the ex-smokers they know. Acting morally superior to someone with a problem is unlikely to lead to a solution to that problem. Few of us respond positively to being told what terrible, immoral people we are.

Exercises
3-2.   Ask people currently working in or receiving human services to describe situations in which they observed someone:
   a.   Blaming the victim
   b.   Acting morally superior

Values for the Human Services

The type of service offered as a solution for a problem will vary depending on the nature of the problem. However, in the authors' opinion, there are some underlying values we feel should guide all human services. Values in human services can be defined as rules governing how to interact with clients and how to design effective services. Following are the values the authors regard as particularly important for the human services professional.

THE PROACTIVE APPROACH TO HUMAN SERVICES

Most of the human service systems in the United States are largely reactive in nature. A problem occurs and we try to solve it. People get sick, so we try to cure them. Crimes are committed, so we try to punish or rehabilitate the offenders. People with chronic mental illnesses are institutionalized, so we try to deinstitutionalize them. These are natural reactions; after all, if your house was on fire, you would try to put out the fire. However, if you want to not only solve the problem, but also prevent it from occurring again in the future, reactive solutions are not enough: you need to design *proactive* solutions. A proactive approach to human problems is one that involves anticipating and preventing problems before they happen (Bernstein, Ziarnik, Rudrud, & Czajkowski, 1981; Ziarnik, 1980).

Proactive human services that seek to prevent problems are becoming more popular. However, this approach is still not used as widely as it might be. That is partly because we are used to reacting to problems instead of preventing them. It is also partly because we are still not as skilled in planning such programs as we might be: we still have a great deal to learn about designing effective and proactive human services. The result is that a program may be only partially proactive.

An example of a partially proactive human service is one that identifies parents who are at risk for becoming abusive and that teaches them nonabusive ways to handle their children. In contrast, a completely proactive approach to child abuse would involve teaching people how to be nonviolent parents *before* they have children.

RESULTS-ORIENTED

"There are a host of anxieties for which the best treatment is rubbing dollar bills all over your body.**"**

(Goodman, 1981, p. 23)

Most of us want to be caring and understanding human services professionals. However, caring is no substitute for results. People who are hungry need food much more than they need understanding. People who are out of work are going to improve their financial picture and their self-esteem by getting jobs, not by getting counseling. It is therefore important to always focus your efforts on results. A wonderful story about a physician who did just that was reported in the January, 1979 issue of *Fortune* magazine:

> Dr. Jack Geiger . . . started the Mound Bayou Health Center in Mississippi . . . Dr. Geiger wrote prescriptions for food to deal with widespread hunger and nutritional deficiencies. Since the Center was established, he estimates infant mortality in the target area has been reduced by almost two-thirds, but Dr. Geiger gives most of the credit to environmental improvements. "If I could do just one thing to improve the health of the people," he says, "I would double their per capita income."

In lectures, Dr. Geiger gleefully tells of the Washington bureaucrats who descended on this clinic protesting that he could not prescribe food. He replied that the diagnosis was hunger—what else could the remedy be? (Neuhauser, 1982, pp. 154–155)

It can be difficult for human services professionals to be primarily concerned with results rather than process. Sometimes the results people need are expensive or threatening in other ways to people with power, or people invested in the status quo, so that these results are difficult to achieve. Sometimes the results people need are straightforward, as in the example described above. In such instances, it can be difficult for human services workers to admit that the needed solutions are simple. It is "hard on the ego to not be able to give the service we want, and hard to admit meaningful solutions are simpler than we try to make them" (C. Learned, personal communication, October 27, 1986).

EMPOWERING

"Sin No. 92: Preventing anyone from growing up."
(Bracken, 1969, p. 138)

" We want to emphasize again that we do not see it as
the function of any therapist to make decisions for the client."
(Corey, Corey, & Callanan, 1988, p. 300)

A human services agency that operates on the notion that it is helping individuals regarded as poor unfortunates is unlikely to encourage people to help themselves. It can make us feel wonderful to give a hungry person food. However, the giving of food is a temporary solution. A more lasting solution is one that helps the individual to learn how to obtain food for him- or herself. This is the difference between parenting and helping. If you feed people forever, they are forever dependent. If you help them to feed themselves, they will not always need human services to take care of them.

Many groups of people formerly thought to be forever dependent are now insisting on becoming sufficiently powerful and independent to care for themselves. For example, numerous people with severe physical disabilities have taken this position. In the last 20 years, independent living centers have been established all over the country. These centers are run partly or completely by people with physical disabilities. Such centers are established to help individuals with severe disabilities to live and work in local communities, instead of living in nursing homes or other restrictive settings.

FREE FROM COERCION

"No one likes being told how to run his affairs."

(Rothman, 1981, p. 180)

It can be hard to accept the fact that some of the people we want to help do not want our help. However, most of the people we want to help have the right to refuse our services. The only exceptions to this rule are those individuals who are dangerous to themselves or to others. Such persons would include drunk drivers, abusive parents, and people with mental illnesses who are dangerous to themselves. In such cases, judges can order that services be administered. Otherwise, services cannot be forced on anyone.

Some of the reasons an individual might choose to reject a service include: it is in conflict with the person's moral or religious standards; it is too costly in terms of time, money, or effort required; it might have undesirable side effects; it might restrict the individual's freedom; it simply is not wanted. One possible response to objections such as these is to redesign your service. That topic is beyond the scope of this book. However, do keep in mind that services can sometimes be made less costly for, and more compatible with, the needs of consumers.

SENSITIVE TO DIVERSITY

"Ignorance is not bad faith. But persistence in ignorance is surely bad faith, from "I'm too tired and don't want to think about it" to "This is interfering with my view of the world so I won't think about it" to "This is interfering with my view of the world which is the only possible and all-inclusive one, so I needn't think about it."

(Russ, 1983, p.46)

American society comprises diverse cultures, religions, and value systems. One of the hard questions facing any human services professional is that of determining a way to solve a particular social problem that is both effective and considerate of this cultural diversity.

The recent news coverage of efforts to stop the spread of AIDS provides an example of the ways in which diverse values affect decisions about solving social problems. For example, the Catholic Church and other religious groups are encouraging abstinence as a way to achieve this objective. Other medical, religious, and political groups are suggesting it is necessary to educate individuals who continue to be sexually active about specific ways to reduce exposure to AIDS. The Catholic Church is opposed to such education. This disagreement is clearly related to diverse moral and religious convictions within our society.

People and organizations are being insensitive to diversity when they assume that their way of doing things is the "normal" way and that everyone they serve should try to be more "normal." Following are some of the ways you can increase your sensitivity to diverse cultures, values, and norms:

1. Find out who you serve. Determine whether the people you serve are members of cultural, religious, or ethnic groups with which you are unfamiliar.
2. Examine the schedule for your agency to determine if it accommodates the people you serve. For instance, is the schedule sensitive to holidays important to consumers of your services?
3. If you serve people who speak limited English and are fluent in another language, find out if any of your staff speak that language.
4. Consider: how diverse is your staff with respect to gender, ethnicity, age, disability, and sexual orientation?
5. Encourage a good working relationship between your agency and local community groups that represent the interests of specific ethnic, religious, or other diverse groups.
6. Examine the reading material in your agency's waiting rooms and the pictures on its walls. Are the people you serve represented in the magazines in the waiting rooms and in the art hanging in the public areas of the agency?
7. Consider whether any of the goals of your agency are in conflict with the values of any of the people you serve. Do you have enough information to answer this question? If there is a conflict, how is your agency dealing with that conflict? (adapted from Nicoloff, 1985)

Exercises
3-3. Describe the human service in which you work or hope to work. What information do you have that tells you whether this service is:
    a. Proactive?
    b. Results-oriented?
    c. Empowering?
    d. Sensitive to diversity?

3-4. Ask someone who works in your chosen form of human services what that service does to be sensitive to diversity. Address the considerations described in the preceding list.

3-5. Review the seven ways to increase sensitivity to diversity described in the list. Identify up to three methods that are needed in your workplace or school and develop a plan for implementing at least one of them.

CONFLICTS ABOUT VALUES IN HUMAN SERVICES

" . . . knowing *how* to change behavior and
knowing *what* to change are two separate issues."

(Duncan & Lloyd, 1982, p. 401)

Human services professionals are expected to be specially skilled in solving certain social problems. For example, it is assumed they know how to change behavior, counsel, provide therapy, and connect people with needed resources. Often, however, public laws and outdated policies dictate the goals of the service professional. Sometimes personal opinions about desirable social goals do not agree with the goals set by the agencies that employ these professionals.

For instance, you might work for a public health agency as a social worker. Suppose the agency requires that anyone who comes in to be tested for a sexually transmitted disease give his or her name. Now suppose you feel more people will come in for testing and treatment if they can be tested anonymously. What do you do?

Often, the goals of social programs are determined by budget decisions. For example, federal legislators decide how much to spend on various national programs. Their decisions determine priorities for all publicly funded human services across the country. Specifically, the amount of money allocated for a particular program determines how many staff the program can afford to hire, as well as how much it can spend on other resources such as buildings and materials.

More specific budget decisions made by program administrators also determine the policies of particular agencies. A school superintendent, for example, has to decide how much to allocate to each specialized program, such as gifted children's classes. A prison director has to decide how much to allocate to new buildings, educational programs, or salaries.

Returning to the subject of policy issues: there is no right or wrong answer to the question of how to handle policy disagreements you have with your employer. If the disagreement is extreme, you may wish to resign rather than live with a policy you oppose. Less drastic measures might include lobbying with your administration and/or congressional representatives for a change in the policy. One may do this individually or through a political action or advocacy group. All American citizens have the opportunity to contribute to decisions about social policy.

Exercises

3-6. If you are currently working in human services, how do you deal with your disagreements, if any, with your agency's policies? If you are currently a student, ask one of your instructors to invite human services professionals to your class to discuss this question.

MORE TALES OF DISILLUSIONED DIANA

Several weeks later: Diana and several friends meet at her apartment. She has been sharing *"Human services? . . . That must be so rewarding"* with them and now they meet once a month to talk through the exercises, their experiences, and to give each other support.

Dave, a friend of Diana's who works in a foster care program, says: "Tonight's exercises really hit home. I had a major disagreement with my supervisor over the agency's policy of re-placing children with abusive parents who show no signs of change after 6 months. I know these kids are at risk for being seriously injured."

The group's conversation escalates into a heated discussion of this policy. Finally Diana asks: "What can we or Dave do"? After more discussion, Dave decides to approach his supervisor in a more rational way than he has in the past, since his ranting and raving earlier had not worked. He plans to ask for support in getting the policy changed through educating policymakers. Diana and the other group members offer to lend support and voices as concerned citizens.

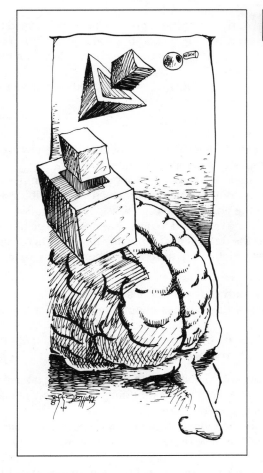

HUMAN

SERVICES

PROFESSIONAL

IN PERSPECTIVE

Most of this book concerns the things human services workers need to do to be effective. However, no one works in a vacuum. Before proceeding to the specifics of this unit, consider the context in which human services professionals work.

The competent, motivated human services professional needs three things in order to be effective. They are:

1. INFORMATION. We need to know:
   a. The goal of the agency where we work. What is the agency supposed to accomplish? What are its values?
   b. Our responsibilities. What are we supposed to accomplish? How are these accomplishments supposed to contribute to achievement of the goals of the organization?
   c. The methods we are expected to use. How are we to go about working toward the desired accomplishments? Are there certain approaches which are required and others which we may not use?

2. RESOURCES. The resources we have consist of:
   a. Our skills. Most of this book is about some of the skills we need.
   b. Materials. Several of the more familiar examples include: buildings, food, library materials, and a telephone.

3. CONSEQUENCES. We have to know whether the things we do make any difference, and we need rewards for doing a good job. Specifically, the consequences we need are:
   a. Feedback. We all need clear, frequent, and specific feedback that tells us what we have done well and what we need to do differently.
   b. Rewards. The most common reward in the human services is praise for doing a good job. It can come from consumers of your services, your supervisors, or your colleagues. Few of us feel good about our work without some sort of reward.

(Gilbert, 1978)

Most of this book concerns resources, but resources alone are not enough. No matter how good your skills are, you still need good information and sufficient consequences in order to be effective. The best time to evaluate whether you have enough information to do a good job is when you are interviewing (see Chapter 7, this volume). The question of whether sufficient consequences are available will come up in our discussion of interviewing and again in Section 4 on Stress Management.

CHAPTER 4

PROFESSIONAL RELATIONSHIPS

OR

People Who Need People

OBJECTIVES

To be able to:

1. Identify and give examples of the fundamentals of good relationships with consumers.
2. Identify and give examples of the fundamentals of good relationships with other staff in your agency.
3. Identify and give examples of the fundamentals of good relationships with other agencies.

Every effective human services professional is skilled at developing and maintaining good relationships with a wide variety of people. This is not surprising, for most human services work involves people and how they interact. Training in the human services tends to focus on relationships with consumers of services, and with good reason. However, if one is to be effective in serving people, one also needs skills in working effectively with colleagues, supervisors, and professionals from other agencies. This chapter outlines several of the fundamentals of those relationships (see Chapter 6, this volume, for a discussion of communication issues in working relationships).

A SAD STORY

The Helpful Home is a residence for six adults with developmental disabilities. The direct care staff are grossly underpaid and overburdened with responsibilities. The program director, Mr. I.M. Torgerson, is giving a tour of the home to Dr. Vera Gardner. He says, as they walk in the door: "I'm sure you can appreciate the difficulty this facility presents for me from a supervision standpoint, as it's located several miles from my office. We try to deal with those problems by having very detailed procedures that the staff must follow." He walks her through the dining room, where staff are gathered, without introducing them. As the tour proceeds, staff are heard grumbling in the background in response.

I.M. goes on: "Some of the residents have some fairly serious self-stimulatory behaviors; some of these behaviors are self-injurious. Sam, here, for example" (he goes to Sam and walks him over to Dr. Gardner) "often flaps his hands to self-stimulate" (while he is talking, Sam starts to flap his hands). "Of course, we use all the latest treatment techniques to deal with this serious problem."

I.M. and the doctor go off to view resident bedrooms, while Sam starts to flap more wildly, and begins beating on himself.

Working Relationships: General Guidelines

Human services professionals who are good at maintaining positive relationships possess five crucial characteristics.

They Treat Everyone with Respect and Common Courtesy They remember to take the time to thank people when it is appropriate, to listen carefully, to be polite even to people who are rude to them, and to be polite to those with whom they disagree (for a more detailed and humorous description of the basics of common courtesy, see *Miss Manners' Guide to Excruciatingly Correct Behavior*). One of the most important components of this characteristic is that they return phone calls as quickly as possible.

They Do What They Say They Will Do They follow through on commitments. If for some reason they are unable to follow through, they tell you that there is a problem and make an attempt to compensate for their failure. They are reliable: they are on time for appointments and meetings. If they will be late, they call and tell you as far in advance as possible.

They Are Proactive They focus their efforts on how to anticipate and solve problems, or parts of problems, before they happen, rather than on how awful things are and how many problems they cannot solve. In the process, they emphasize strengths in people and organizations.

They Check Their Facts They do not rely on hearsay or gossip, and they routinely obtain information from several different sources before taking a position on an issue.

They Are Accountable for What They Do   They acknowledge their failures as well as their successes. When they make mistakes, they admit to them and learn from them.

Exercises

4-1.   Analyze "A Sad Story." What is wrong with the relationships described in it?

4-2.   Describe how a human services worker who works well with others would handle each of the following situations:

   a.   A disgruntled service consumer calls and says: "You social service types are all the same. Lots of promises about helping people, but you never deliver."

   b.   Your supervisor unexpectedly tells you there is a meeting of the entire staff in 2 hours which you must attend. You have already scheduled a meeting at that time with staff from two other agencies.

   c.   A parole officer from another agency calls and tells you he has heard that an individual you both serve is starting to miss work and use drugs. He is calling to say he is ready to report this person for parole violations.

   d.   One of your colleagues constantly complains that there is so much paperwork to do, she cannot do a good job of providing services. You have noticed that there do seem to be a large number of forms to fill out.

   e.   You missed the deadline for submitting an important document. Consequently, one of the people you serve will not get some badly needed financial support for another month.

Sample Solutions

4-2.   a.   Take a deep breath. Allow the irritated consumer to vent. As the person's speech starts to slow down, try to paraphrase the problem. For instance, you might say: "You have not received your unemployment check yet, and it is the 10th of the month. I can understand why you are upset. Let me check into the delay and call you back by 2:00 P.M." This solution treats the consumer with respect, promises follow-through, and allows you to check the facts.

   b.   Explain your conflict to your supervisor. If you are told you must be at the staff meeting, call the other agencies. Explain that an emergency meeting has been called that is mandatory, make a sincere apology, and ask to either have the meeting go on without you or to have it rescheduled. If the meeting will be rescheduled, be ready to provide specific times you are available. Repeat your apology and end the conversation. Do not refer to your supervisor or the emergency meeting as inflexible or unreasonable, even if they are. This solution is proactive: it allows you to maintain a positive relationship with your supervisor and the other agencies.

Working with Consumers

Some critically important aspects of working with people receiving services are addressed in Chapter 2. To review briefly, they are:

1. Remember that the people we serve are *people first.* Remember to acknowledge their strengths and contributions as well as their needs.
2. Everyone has *the right to be taken seriously.* Everyone has the right to be treated with respect.
3. *Fit the solution to the problem.* Do not assume one type of solution will work for every problem.
4. Choose the *least intrusive solution to any problem.* This means solutions should be inexpensive, accessible, and compatible with the person's values, and as noninvasive of privacy as possible.

In addition to these fundamental guidelines for working with consumers of human services, there are several other considerations, such as courtesy and confidentiality, that deserve our attention.

THE NEED FOR COMMON COURTESY

One of the best comments we have found concerning the ways human services professionals should act and sometimes do not was made by Carolyn L. Vash. Dr. Vash is a psychologist who also has a physical disability. She has been both a provider and a consumer of human services. She recently wrote that much of the difficulty in evaluation units comes from " . . . failures of common courtesy and overconcern about one's own busy schedule at the expense of the client's time" (Vash, 1984, p. 256). The authors would add that these problems are common to all human services, not just evaluation units. Dr. Vash continues:

> Most of our parents taught us better behavior, but somehow we forget. Rudeness sometimes begins the moment the client arrives. We do not introduce him to the other people present. We do not show him where to put his coat. We do not tell him where the restroom is. . . We do not offer

him a cup of coffee. . . When shy people who fear the worst attend social functions in our homes, we usually take the time and make special efforts to reassure and welcome them. When people who are scared to death visit our facilities, comparable efforts are in order (Vash, 1984, pp. 256–257).

Exercises

4-3   Use your own experience and/or interviews with other human services professionals to:
   a.   Identify five examples of failures by human services workers to use common courtesy with consumers of service.
   b.   Identify five examples of good use of common courtesy by human services workers when interacting with consumers of service.

ON CONFIDENTIALITY

Most human services workers are privy to intimate information about the people they serve. While the details of confidentiality laws and regulations may vary from state to state and from service type to service type, the fundamentals remain the same. We are required to keep private information private unless there is a possibility of danger; in such cases, the law requires us to report the information. This means we cannot talk about the people we serve by name or reveal other identifying information to anyone not involved directly in service delivery to those people. Furthermore, we cannot talk to any professional from another human services agency about an individual being served unless a signed release of information is obtained from the consumer, that person's parent (if the consumer is underage), or from the legal guardian. If a consumer of services is an adult and has not been declared incompetent, that person must agree and sign a release before information is shared with *anyone,* including spouses, parents, and other relatives. This does not mean professionals are prohibited from seeking consultation on how to improve what they do. However, if professionals consult with anyone outside of their agencies, they are required to describe the situation without identifying the person involved.

The one standard exception to the rules on releasing confidential information is when people receiving services request that you release their records. Most of the time a signed written release is required which tells what information can be released, to whom, and within what time period. In that instance, professionals are obligated to carry out the client's wishes. (Sometimes it is unclear whether an individual is competent to give consent. For a discussion of this issue, see Barber, 1980; Rosoff, 1981; Turnbull, 1977; Woody, 1984.)

Exercises

4-4. Determine which of the following is a breach of confidentiality:

   a. A colleague from your agency who serves the same people as you calls and asks if you know anything about an individual you are serving. You give him the information requested.

   b. The father of a 22-year-old man who is receiving services from your organization calls to see how he is doing. You tell him.

   c. A staff member from a nearby independent living center calls and asks for information about someone you served last month. You provide the information.

   d. On the elevator to your office, one of your colleagues says: "Hey, how's Sally Smith doing? I've heard she is making excellent progress." Your colleague also provides services to Sally Smith.

   e. You leave a confidential file on your desk while you go to lunch.

   f. You take a phone call in a colleague's office and it is about someone you serve.

Answers to Exercise

Answers (b) and (c) are definite breaches of confidentiality unless the father and the independent living center staff have obtained signed releases of information from the people receiving services. Answer (a) is not a breach because you both work for the same agency and provide services to the same person. Answer (d) is not a breach *if no one else is on the elevator.* Answer (e) is a breach waiting to happen because the opportunity exists for someone unauthorized to read the file. Answer (f) depends on whether your colleague stays in the office, and on whether your colleague is also serving the person you discuss on the phone.

ON SEXUAL COERCION

Human services workers are almost always in positions that give them power over the people they serve. Sometimes that power is overt, as when a social worker has the power to decide whether an individual is eligible for a particular type of benefit. Sometimes the power is less obvious, as when a counselor has the power to help someone decide how to solve a personal problem. Even though many laws exist that protect the rights of people receiving services, those people may be too frightened, troubled, or unaware of their rights to exercise them.

This imbalance of power carries with it a special responsibility to refrain from abusing that power. This responsibility applies especially with respect to sexual relations. *It is always unethical, and usually illegal, to engage in sexual relations with anyone receiving services from you. In fact, the authors call the involvement of any human services worker in a sexual relationship with a current consumer of their services "professional rape."* This may seem so obvious to you that it goes without saying, but the authors have seen it happen in a variety of different situations. There is no excuse for engaging in a sexual relationship with someone you are serving as a human services professional. We have seen human services professionals who were confused and were having personal problems of their own engage in sexual relationships with people they serve. This is unfortunate and unacceptable. We have also seen human services professionals deliberately take sexual advantage of the people they are supposedly serving. This is also unacceptable, and should be grounds for immediate termination of the worker and possible legal action.

Exercises

4-5. Using your own experience and observations, or those of other human services professionals in your field, identify five ways in which a human service professional could coerce a consumer of services into a sexual relationship.

4-6. Describe what your ethical and legal obligations are if you discover that one of your colleagues is engaging in a sexual relationship with a consumer of services.

EMPOWERMENT AND CONTROL

In Chapter 3, the authors proposed empowerment as a major value for the human services. This means we help people to take control of their own lives, rather than telling them what to do. One way to act on this value is to focus your efforts on helping people to arrive at their own decisions. It is particularly difficult for us to step back and help people make their own decisions when we strongly favor one choice in particular. Some difficult decisions it may be hard to help people make for themselves are:

Whether a pregnant 15-year-old should have an abortion
Whether a battered woman should leave her husband
Whether a retarded man should take a job that pays well doing work
    he does not like
Whether a physically disabled individual should walk everywhere

with difficulty instead of using a wheelchair, which makes mobility easier.

Helping people to make their own decisions instead of telling them what to do is not easy. It is usually more time-consuming than telling them what to do, particularly if you are serving people who do not have much practice at making their own decisions. Teaching decision-making, depending on the skills the learner already has, can involve one or more of the following steps:

1. Figure out that there is a decision to be made.
2. Generate several possible decisions from which to choose.
3. Analyze possible outcomes of each decision.
4. Choose the decision most likely to satisfy the decision maker.

If one of your values is empowerment, you may need to learn to teach decision-making skills to the people you serve (see, for example, D'Zurilla, 1987). Also, you need to be able to monitor yourself and look for ways in which you help people decide, as well as ways in which you hinder independent decision-making.

Human services professionals who wish to empower the people they serve must not only avoid telling service consumers what to do, but they must also avoid taking too much credit for improvements in people's lives.

> "Some people never catch on to this and will
> insist on showing off what 'they' did—patronizing
> at best, and a great way to make a lifelong enemy. . ."
>
> (Pryor, 1984, p. 81)

We all need to feel in control of our lives, and are unlikely to react well to someone else claiming to have control over us.

Exercises

4-7. How would you respond to each of the following situations so that people will be encouraged make their own decisions?
   a. A student comes to the counseling center and says: "I've always wanted to be an English teacher, but lately I've been having second thoughts. Maybe I should go into business instead."
   b. A man who has been living with a woman and their two children is trying to decide whether to marry her.
   c. A woman comes for help in deciding whether to tell her children that she is a lesbian.

Working with Colleagues: Support Staff

*"Poor planning on your part does
not necessarily constitute an emergency on my part."*

(Anonymous)

There is an old cliché with a lot of truth in it that suggests that the world is really run by secretaries and janitors. Unfortunately, too often secretaries and janitors are treated with little respect and are not seen as professionals. This is unfortunate for several reasons. First, and most important, it is incumbent on us to practice what we preach. If we truly believe that all people are entitled to be treated with respect and to have their contributions to the world acknowledged, we need to behave as if that is true all the time. There is no excuse for being rude to support staff, nor is there any excuse for only acknowledging their contributions to the agency once a year, such as at Christmas time or on Secretary's Day, if at all.

The people who answer your telephones, type your reports, and clean your offices make it possible for you to do your job. They are entitled, as are we all, to recognition for a job well done and to respect and courtesy as a matter of course. Saying "Please" and "Thank you" not only is a recognition of the respect everyone is entitled to, but it also contributes to a more pleasant working atmosphere. Finally, your support staff are probably going to give better service to people who treat them with respect than to people who do not. However, you should not expect special favors just because you are courteous to support staff. For instance, do not expect someone to stay late to type a report you have put off writing until the last minute. This is an abuse of power and an example of expecting someone else to clean up your mess. Further, it is unacceptable behavior on the part of any adult, let alone any human services professional.

Exercises

4-8. Identify three ways to recognize and reward contributions of support staff to your organization throughout the year. Do not use flowers or candy, or anything specific to Secretary's Day.

4-9. Identify three ways to help support staff feel important to, and involved in, organizational planning and operations.

COLLEAGUES

The development of good working relationships with other human services professionals within your agency is one of the most difficult tasks you face. When we work closely with people over a long period of time, they come to know our strengths and our faults well. Similarly, we come to know them equally well. It is easy, but not very useful, to focus on the things our colleagues do badly. We all have characteristics that other people find irritating or frustrating. Some common examples are popping chewing gum, touching you more than you want to be touched, or having a speaking voice that you find too loud or too soft.

An emphasis on your co-workers' strengths is more difficult, but also more rewarding, than an emphasis on their faults. Further, none of us is perfect, so we are probably just as annoying to them as they are to us! One of the ways to build positive working relationships is to look on these relationships as being collaborative (Zins, 1985). In collaborative relationships, each individual contributes in his or her areas of strength and seeks assistance from others who have skills in other areas of strength.

For instance, suppose you are very good at working with people once they come to you for services, but you are not good at going into new situations and effectively letting people know what you have to offer. This is an ideal opportunity to build a collaborative relationship with a colleague who is good at presenting your agency to potential users of services. It is important for other people to feel you need them, and it is important that you not try to act as an expert in everything. No one knows everything, and people who act as if they do are usually treated with hostility and suspicion.

It is particularly important to build good working relationships with your co-workers when your work requires you to be out of the office often. Lack of visibility, which occurs when your colleagues do not have a chance to observe you doing the most important parts of your job, is a frequent problem in human services agencies. This can lead to the assumption that you are not working, and that you "have it easy." This is not because people always look for bad news. If one does not see something and does not hear about it, one tends to assume it does not exist. The solution to this problem is simple: keep people informed about what you do. This is not to be confused with tooting your own horn. People who toot their own horns are interested in letting everyone know how wonderful they are. People who are interested in having good working relationships and keeping colleagues informed make sure their office knows how to reach them when they are out in the field. In addition, they take the time to sit down with a colleague with a mutual interest or overlapping responsibilities and say something like:"I'm involved in a project in which you might be interested. Can I take a few minutes to fill you in"?

Sexual Relationships with Colleagues

When sexual relationships with colleagues develop, some interesting problems in the workplace may result. There is no prohibition against intimate relationships with colleagues in the way that there is against sexual relationships with consumers of services. However, having an intimate relationship with a colleague is still problematic. One issue is that, unless you are both very careful, other colleagues will find out. If you value your privacy, this is a problem. Also, if your colleagues find out about the relationship, they may have reactions you find objectionable. Examples of such reactions might include: the expectation that you will keep them up to date on all the emotional details; jealousy, if you are involved with someone in whom they have an interest; moral condemnation; matchmaking, such as trying to push the relationship into more intimacy and commitment than is desired. Another consideration is that you will still have to work with each other if the relationship ends. This can be very awkward.

The potential for moral condemnation is likely and can create considerable unpleasantness. The chances that everyone in your organization shares the same values regarding personal relationships are not high. Thus a relationship that you find rewarding may be seen by others as sinful, unprofessional, or in bad taste. Should this occur, do not count on colleagues who hold these opinions to keep them a secret. This is particularly true if you are a woman. While social values have changed, women are still judged more harshly than men for similar behavior. This is not desirable, but it is real and you need to be prepared for it.

The same admonition applies even more if your intimate relationships are with members of the same sex. Again, while some social values have changed, lesbians and gay men are still more likely to encounter condemnation for their social lives than are their heterosexual colleagues.

The authors are not suggesting that your social life never include your co-workers. It is usually not possible to divide life into such clean, neat categories. However, we are suggesting that you remember the potential for problems when the irresistible woman or man in the next office asks you out for dinner.

Exercises

4-10. a. Identify five characteristics of your own which your colleagues might find irritating or unacceptable.
 b. Identify five characteristics of current or future colleagues which you find irritating or unacceptable.
 c. Consider: How do you want your colleagues to deal with your quirks?
 d. Consider: How should you deal with theirs?
4-11. Describe three ways in which you could demonstrate respect for a colleague's skills.

SUPERVISORS

On Being Supervised

Our supervisors connect us with the organizations where we work. It is probably harder to develop a good relationship with your supervisor than with any other colleague. Most of us have some difficulty in our relationships with people in positions of authority. Working with supervisors can be touchy because they are responsible for evaluating your performance.

There are ways you can act if you want to have a positive relationship with your supervisor, and ways your supervisor can work positively with you. The supervisory relationship does not have to be a negative one.

Your Obligations to Your Supervisor

1. Keep your supervisor informed about what you are doing, and about any events that may be important to your organization.
2. If you have a complaint about your organization, take it to your supervisor, not your colleagues. And remember, your supervisor may not agree with you, or may not be able to solve the problem as quickly as you would like, or may not be able to solve it at all.
3. Behave as, and expect to be treated as, a professional, not a child. Supervisors are not parents.
4. Treat your supervisor with respect. It helps to like the people you work with, but it is not essential. Treating your supervisor and your colleagues with respect is essential.
5. Give your supervisor positive and corrective feedback on how you are being supervised. Remember to use diplomacy. Be aware that all supervisors may not be open to corrective feedback.

6. Remember your supervisor is your supervisor, with responsibilities both to you and the organization. Expect your supervisor to have a professional relationship with you, not a close friendship.

Following are two helpful ways to approach developing a positive relationship with your supervisor.

First, treat your supervisor like a consumer. Use tact and timing in presenting issues to your supervisor, just as you would with an important consumer. If your supervisor gives you feedback you do not fully understand, ask for clarification. Use the type of communication (e.g., memo, face-to-face meeting) and schedule for communicating preferred by your supervisor (Scott, 1980).

Second, try to see things from your supervisor's perspective: try to mirror your supervisor's need to see the big picture. Be sensitive to the fact that there are multiple demands on the supervisor's time, and every little detail of your daily work is not of interest to him or her. Prepare carefully for meetings with your supervisor. Try to present issues and reports that cover important points as briefly as possible (and be prepared to provide more detail in case it is requested). If you have problems to present, be prepared to suggest at least one solution. Even if your solution is not used, the fact that you have provided one shows that you are committed to being an active part of the problem-solving process (Murphy, 1987).

On Being a Supervisor If you make human services your career for an extended period of time, you will almost certainly become a supervisor. Just as you have obligations to the person who is your supervisor, you have obligations to the people you supervise.

Your Obligations to the People You Supervise

1. Be accessible.
2. Practice what you preach. If your staff are expected to treat service consumers and colleagues with respect and with some understanding of their problems, they have a right to receive similar treatment from their supervisor.
3. Make clear what is expected of your staff professionally. These expectations should be tempered by a realistic view of available resources (McInerney, 1985).
4. Treat your staff with respect, even when they disagree with you (McInerney, 1985).
5. Give staff members regular, specific feedback about work performance. This does not refer to semiannual or annual reviews, but

rather to ongoing daily or weekly comments about what they are doing well and what needs improvement. They also have the right to expect recognition for a job well done.

6. Everyone you supervise has the right to be allowed to make mistakes and to learn from them (McInerney, 1985).

7. Guarantee the right to confidentiality regarding supervision, particularly when receiving constructive criticism (McInerney, 1985). Effective supervisors provide praise in public and constructive criticism in private.

Working with Other Agencies

It is impossible to work in human services without having contact with other human services agencies. This is because no one agency ever completely meets an individual's needs. Hence, comprehensive assistance requires services from more than one source. Communication and collaboration with other service agencies are part of our daily lives.

Effective working relationships with other agencies are important for several reasons. They allow us to share information about effective service strategies within the confines of confidentiality requirements. When we can call colleagues at other agencies and quickly find additional services for an individual, we are saving the time and energy of the consumer of services. Good working relationships also allow us to identify gaps in available services that can be brought to the attention of policymakers.

Good working relationships with other agencies can be difficult to establish and maintain. One reason for this difficulty is that the focus of one agency's efforts may be different from those of another agency. Vocational training programs, for instance, are focused on getting people employed, while child protective services may be primarily interested in the welfare of the children of vocational trainees.

There are several steps that can be taken to promote good working relationships with other agencies. First, adopt the five characteristics of the competent human services professional described at the beginning of this chapter. Specifically:

1. Treat everyone with respect and common courtesy. Even if you are dealing with someone whom you have good reason to consider incompetent or devious, failure to treat that person with courtesy is unlikely to improve the situation.

2. Do what you say you will do, and let people know if something prevents you from doing it.
3. Be proactive: praise other agencies for what they do for people. Avoid criticizing them for what they do not do. They are probably more familiar with their limitations than you are. Remember that all human services organizations are chronically short of staff and money, and therefore limited in what they can do. Focus on the needs of the people you serve, and on ways your agency and other agencies can join forces to meet those needs.
4. Check your facts. If you hear that someone from another agency has described your actions incorrectly, do not call and say: "I'm very upset with what you said about how I handled Mr. Johnson's request for services, you so-and-so"! Instead, call that person and say: "I need to check with you about a report I received today: I've been told you said some things about my response to Mr. Johnson that are incorrect, and I want to check with you directly rather than rely on hearsay."
5. Be accountable. Acknowledge your failures as well as your successes. We all know that no one is perfect and that no agency is perfect: if we try to hide our imperfections we look silly and dishonest.

Two additional tactics are extremely useful when working with other agencies:

1. Communicate clearly about what your job is, what your agency does, and what your agency does not do. Too often we assume that the rest of the world knows exactly what is available from our agency and what is not. This assumption is usually incorrect.
2. Develop good negotiating skills. This is essential; when you work with other agencies, you have no direct authority over them. Thus, you need to negotiate with those agencies rather than dictate to them. Negotiation is discussed extensively in Section 4.

Exercises

4-12. For each of the following situations, provide at least two ways to respond. Give responses that are likely to lead to a solution of the problem and likely to maintain a good relationship with the other agency involved.
   a. You are an independent living skills trainer for people with physical disabilities. One of the people you have been serving for some

time announces that he is withdrawing from your program because his social worker told him the government will take care of him for the rest of his life, so he does not have to learn to do anything for himself.

b. You are a teacher of emotionally disturbed children. A representative from a local advocacy organization calls you on behalf of the Cohens, who are parents of one of the children you teach. The representative states that the Cohens want to have a special meeting to talk about improving the educational services being provided for their daughter. They feel the present program is not meeting their child's needs.

Possible Solutions

4-12. a. You might agree it is true his government benefits will continue. Talk to him briefly about the self-worth many people gain from increasing ability to care for themselves (do not preach). Then give him your card and tell him you will be glad to talk to him again if he changes his mind. Remember you have no way of knowing whether he is quoting his social worker accurately, so call that person and matter-of-factly report what happened and ask if the quote is accurate. If it is an accurate quote, you may want to disagree, but do it directly to the social worker, not indirectly through the gossip mill.

b. Check with the Cohens and make sure they have authorized the advocate to represent them. Agree to have the requested meeting with the Cohens. Prepare for the meeting by summarizing the data you have concerning the child's identified needs and what the school program is doing for this child. Finally, listen carefully at the meeting before responding at all.

NEGOTIATION

"Sin No. 16: Being too positive your way is the only way."

(Bracken, 1969, p. 74)

"A wise agreement can be defined as one which meets the legitimate interests of each side to the extent possible, resolves conflicting interests fairly, is durable, and takes community interests into account." (Fisher & Ury, 1981, p. 4)

The dictionary defines *negotiate* as a verb meaning "to confer, bargain, or discuss with a view to reaching agreement" (Webster's New World Dictionary, 1962, p. 982). Thus, any conversations we have with other people that are intended to result in delivery of some human service are forms of negotiation. *Principled negotiation,* a process described by Fisher and Ury (1981) of the Harvard Negotiation Project, can be particularly useful. Principled negotiation is concerned with both the *substance* and the *process* of negotiation. The concern with substance ensures that the result of a negotiation will, as much as possible, meet the legitimate interests of all those involved. The concern with process ensures that the negotiation process and its outcome will not damage the relationship between the persons involved (Fisher & Ury, 1981).

The Substance of Negotiation

Principled negotiation focuses on the interests or principles of the people involved, instead of on the people themselves or on particular positions. The intent is to find a solution consistent with the values of all concerned. In this way, it is possible for all negotiating parties to be winners; no one must lose.

The Process of Negotiation

Principled negotiation assumes that the process by which you arrive at an agreement is as important as the substance of the agreement. If you want people to implement an agreed upon solution to a problem, you must ensure that they feel the solution is fair, and you must ensure they feel they were important to the design of the solution. Here are some ways to make the negotiation process an effective one:

Use the Language of Social Cohesion Unoriginal remarks such as: "How about this weather"? or "Did you catch that game last night"? may sound silly to you, but they serve several purposes. First, they establish a connection between people, so that when serious negotiations begin, those involved do not feel like they are dealing with strangers. Also, they serve to establish a positive connection by allowing people who may later disagree or become angry with each other to discuss neutral, all-purpose topics. They keep communication open: even when substantive discussions are at a standstill, people can stay in contact by discussing yesterday's record snowfall. Finally, unoriginal remarks can be useful because they prevent silence, and many people are uncomfortable with silence (Hayakawa, 1964).

Make Sure Everyone Participates so that Everyone Will Have a Stake in the Solution "If they are not involved in the process, they are hardly likely to approve the product" (Fisher & Ury, 1981, p. 27). Negotiation must be approached without a specific solution in mind that is the only solution you will accept. Certainly, you will have some ideas about what is at stake and possible ways to proceed, but the other parties to the negotiation will also have ideas about what to do. The negotiation process should provide ways to combine those ideas and to find a solution acceptable to all concerned.

Show Appreciation for the Difficulties of the Other Parties (Zins, 1985) You may take it for granted that you understand the pressures and constraints felt by others, but they will not know you understand unless you tell them. For instance, you might say to the single parent: "It must be difficult for you to arrange to bring Sally in for regular therapy and still manage your work schedule and your son's after school activities." Or, you might say to the rehabilitation counselor who works for the state office: "It sounds like you feel the bureaucratic requirements you need to meet will slow down the service delivery process." Note that in this example, you acknowledge the counselor's position without necessarily agreeing with it. People with whom you disagree need to know that you have heard them, even if you then disagree. Other parties to a negotiation will not listen if you ignore any expression with which you disagree.

Arrange a Physical Environment that Fosters Cooperation For instance, it can help if two parties with differing interests sit on the same side of the table (Fisher & Ury, 1981). Round tables can also help. Avoid like the plague any arrangement that puts the consumer and her or his representatives on one side of a table and all the service providers on the other side. Such an arrangement suggests that people have chosen sides, and can make them more likely to behave as enemies.

Explain Your Interests and Ask for Theirs Do not assume they understand your primary interest, and, even more important, do not assume you understand theirs. For instance, suppose you work in a residential treatment program for emotionally disturbed children. One of the children has made considerable progress and you are ready to recommend a less restrictive treatment setting (probably his home) to his parents. In the meeting with them you say: "My primary interest here is in finding a way for Jake to move to a less restrictive setting. We think he can function very well in his home school with consultation to the teacher and family by the therapist. You seem pleased with Jake's progress, but reluctant to move him home. Could I ask you to describe your concerns"?

Identify the Problem Before Identifying the Answer Perhaps the single most important barrier to problem solving in human services is the tendency of many of us to assume we know what the problem is and therefore assume the solution is obvious. In fact, many of the disagreements we observe in interdisciplinary or cross-agency meetings are due to differing assumptions about the nature of a problem. For instance, suppose Joan Garcia, who has been labeled chronically mentally ill, frequently comes to work and sits and cries. Possible explanations and solutions are: 1) she is frustrated because the job is too hard, so she needs easier work, 2) she is getting lots of supervisor attention for crying and should get more attention for working and less for crying, and 3) her husband is abusing her and she needs to move to a battered women's shelter.

Suppose Joan, her social worker, and a vocational rehabilitation counselor meet and discover that each believes a different one of the explanations and solutions given above. If each person presents only his or her preferred solution and does not explain the reason for it, agreement is unlikely. If each person presents her or his explanation, all three explanations can be analyzed by everyone involved.

Make Emotions Explicit and Legitimate   Nearly all human services negotiations involve strong emotions, because people's lives are the subject of the discussions. It would be silly to ignore those feelings, but it is not productive to let problem-solving sessions dissolve into emotional outpourings.

> One unusual and effective technique to contain the impact of emotions was used in the 1950s by the Human Relations Committee, a labor-management group set up in the steel industry to handle emerging conflicts before they became serious problems. The members of the committee adopted the rule that only one person could get angry at a time. This made it legitimate for others not to respond stormily to an angry outburst. It also made letting off emotional steam easier by making an outburst itself more legitimate: "That's OK. It's his turn."
> (Fisher & Ury, 1981, p. 32)

List All Options First, Then Evaluate   Often the resolution to a problem will be a patchwork of solutions proposed by several different people. That is why it is helpful to lay out all possible options before narrowing them down. Suppose an adolescent who is on probation because he is in trouble with the law suggests as his solution dropping out of school and getting a job. His father might suggest military school, his mother might suggest counseling, and the solution ultimately agreed upon might be a combination of a special school, a part-time job, and counseling.

Consider Multiple Options   Avoid premature judgments, especially avoid searching for a single best answer. Such a solution does not exist. Also avoid the assumption that if one party gets more, the other party inevitably gets less.

Consider the Consequences of the Decision You Request from the Other Party's Perspective For instance, one of the reasons the parents of Jake, the boy described earlier, may be reluctant to bring him home is that one parent has just been laid off and they are not sure they can feed him adequately. Or, they may be concerned about the effect his return will have on their other children. It is important that you help the parents find a solution that not only meets their son's needs, but also speaks to their concerns. If you really want to find a solution, do not assume that solving the parents' dilemma is *their* problem. If you want to find a solution, you should make it your problem, too.

Exercises

4-13. Suppose you are the discharge social worker for a state hospital for persons with mental disabilities. Sylvia Towns, one of your patients, is about to be discharged and needs services and a residence in the community. She has chronic schizophrenia that is controlled by daily medication. She is not dangerous, but she starts hallucinating and loses touch with reality if she does not take her medication regularly. You are about to meet with Ms. Towns, with a representative of a very overworked and understaffed community mental health center, and with Ms. Towns's sister, a single parent with a limited income and two preschool-age children. With three classmates, role-play the meeting intended to establish community services for Ms. Towns. Use the principled negotiation strategies described above.

DIANA'S STORY CONTINUES

One month later, Diana asks: "Dave, what happened when you went back to your boss about changing the policy concerning when to put kids back in abusive homes"?

"Well, you know at first I really dreaded bringing it up again. I had been so out of control before, so upset. I guess it's harder to be calm, rational and professional than to shoot off your mouth. I kept putting off meeting with my boss—had lots of reasons, was very busy, I told myself. In the meantime I worked on the exercises in this chapter. Are they tough"!

Diana and the others in their group start agreeing how hard the chapter and exercises were. As the conversation gets louder, Bob Greene, Diana's good friend from the apartment across the hall, knocks on the door.

When Diana opens the door for Bob, he says: "Diana, what's going on—sounds like a riot. I've noticed you have these loud, angry meetings once a month. Is this some off-the-wall cult"?

Laughing, Diana invites Bob in and introduces the group. Bob is an officer from the local county sheriff's office who works in juvenile crime prevention. When the group explains what it is doing, Bob asks if he can stay and join the discussion. Everyone welcomes Bob, and Kathryn says: "Good, someone else to help us with these exercises"!

Later, Diana remembers Dave's problem, and suggests to the group: "Before you go, Dave never finished telling us what happened with his policy problem."

"Well, after lots of procrastination I spoke with my supervisor. I had typed up some current research findings on child abuse to back up my arguments. It was a little uncomfortable at first, but she heard me out, asked some good questions, and now I'm to head up a task force to present the issue to the agency director in a meeting in 2 months."

Someone says: "So all you got was a brush-off and more work."

"No," Dave replies, "I'm looking at it as a chance to begin to make a change in the system. Well, folks, this was really helpful, but I have to run. Still have some notes to write up tonight. See you next month at my place."

CHAPTER 5

TIME MANAGEMENT

OR

A Time for Every Purpose under the Heaven

OBJECTIVES

To be able to:

1. Assess your time management skills.
2. Analyze how you are currently using your time.
3. Design a plan for improving time management skills.
4. Evaluate how well your time management plan is working.

"A messy desk is only a sign of a messy desk.**"**
(Scott, 1980, p. 172)

"Being busy is not synonymous with being productive.**"**
(Maher & Cook, 1985, p. 41)

We all have time. In fact, there is an old adage that says time is all we have. This chapter is about time and the human services professional. We all have things to do and time to do them in. The challenge is to use time in ways that make us productive, effective, and satisfied with how we have used our time. There are many books and training programs that can help you to improve your time management skills, and most of them have something useful to offer. One of the most useful books we have found is Dr. Dru Scott's *How to Put More Time in Your Life*. Many of her ideas are reflected in this chapter, and we are pleased to acknowledge her work and its influence on our approach.

Exercises

5-1. Consider how effectively you currently manage your professional time. Answer the following questions:
   a. What time management skills do I have? Which of these skills are the strongest?
   b. What time management skills could I improve? How can I make these skills more effective?

Myths about Time and Time Management

There are innumerable myths about how one uses time. Some of the most common are:

I Haven't Got Time to Use All that Time Management Stuff *(Scott, 1980)* This is the perfect excuse for never taking control of your time, and is just plain silly. If you never take a serious look at how you use time and whether there is anything you want to change about how you use time, you have only yourself to blame.

The People I Work with Won't Let Me Manage My Time the Way I Want *(Scott, 1980)* This puts the blame for misuse of your time squarely on other people. You cannot expect your colleagues, your boss, or the people you serve to magically stop interrupting, stop calling at bad times, or stop coming up with new projects for you. However, there are ways to manage these problems. They are discussed in depth later in this chapter.

Time Management is Boring *(Scott, 1980)* There are two responses to this myth. First, does it matter if time management is boring if it gives you what you want? Second, time management is not an "it" which is boring. Instead, it is a process composed of choices about how to use your time. You can choose nonboring ways to manage your time.

How I Manage My Time is Just Part of My Personality Wrong! We use time in certain ways because we have learned to do so, or because there are cues in our working environments for using time in those ways, or because we are getting something out of using time in those ways. You can change how you manage time by learning new skills or by finding ways to change the cues or consequences for your use of time.

If I Use Time Management, My Life Will Be Too Controlled *(Scott, 1980)* First, if you use time management deliberately, *you* will be the person in control of your time. Now, perhaps you equate time management with having every minute scheduled, and you value spontaneity. Time management does not mean your whole life is scheduled in advance! It means routine responsibilities are scheduled and controlled, so you have more free time to be spontaneous and creative.

A STRATEGY FOR TIME MANAGEMENT

One of the major flaws in many books and workshops on time management is that they start by giving you specific techniques for managing your time more efficiently. The technique-centered approach ignores the fact that we are all unique and may have very different problems with time management, and many problems that require individualized solutions. You are more likely to find a solution that works for you if you follow the following steps:

1. Identify your time use goals. This includes what you want to do tomorrow, next week, and next month. Accomplishments might include calls to be made, meetings to attend, or projects to finish.
2. Find out whether you are currently meeting your goals.
3. If you are not meeting your goals, identify what keeps you from meeting them. Identify the barriers that get in the way of your attempts to accomplish what you set out to do.
4. Design and use methods for solving time management problems. For instance, you might decide to only take incoming phone calls in the morning, instead of all day long. Or, you might focus on ending interruptions quickly by saying: "This is a bad time for me right now, when can I get back to you"?
5. Find out if your solutions are effective.

The remainder of this chapter concerns the ways to use these five steps. As you work through the chapter, please remember that time management is an *ongoing* process, not a one-time only activity. Every time there is a change in your work situation, the possibility exists that you will need to review how effectively you are using your time. That does not mean you have failed: it just means that circumstances have changed, so you may have to change with them.

Identifying Time Management Goals

There are two ways of evaluating how a person uses time. One way is to evaluate results. This means we look at what the person has accomplished as a result of what he or she has done. In human services, some of the consumer-related accomplishments we examine might include: whether a jail inmate or juvenile delinquent stays out of trouble after receiving counseling, whether a child has learned to read, whether a

disabled worker has gone back to work, or if a previously dysfunctional family is getting along better. Some other accomplishments we
examine are administrative. These would include: whether paperwork
is up-to-date, if a new assessment tool has been developed, if next
month's food supply for a consumer's home has been ordered.

The second way to evaluate time use is to look at process. In other
words, we look at how time is spent. Typical ways we spend time in
human services include: meeting with consumers of services, meeting
with people from other agencies, and meeting in informal brainstorming sessions with colleagues.

If you are to identify your time use and accomplishment goals,
you need to consider both what you want and what is required of you.
It is important to consider both wants and requirements because they
are seldom identical, though they often overlap. Therefore, the four
questions to ask yourself when you want to identify your time management goals are:

1. What results do I want to achieve?
2. Am I currently achieving my assigned goals?
3. How do I *want* to spend my professional time?
4. How do I *need* to spend my professional time?

Exercises

5-2. It is often useful to identify goals for managing varying periods of time.
Table 1 asks you for your goals for tomorrow, the next week, and the next
month.
  a. If you are currently working in human services, fill out the chart for
  yourself in your current position.
  b. If you are a student and are not currently working in human services, try two uses of the chart. First, fill it out for yourself in your
  role as a student. Second, find someone currently working in human services and ask them if they will fill out the chart and show it
  to you.
5-3. The chart you used for Exercise 5-2 is not the only way to look at how
you spend your time. Another approach is to divide what you do at work
into discretionary and nondiscretionary time (Medved & Burns, 1983).

Nondiscretionary time is time spent reacting to situations or car-
rying out responsibilities assigned to you such as reports, phone calls,
or required meetings. Discretionary time is time over which you have
control. Examples of ways to spend discretionary time at work are:
volunteering for a special task force or participating in a research project of interest to you. Most of us want to manage our nondiscretionary
time in ways that give us as much discretionary time as possible.
  a. If you are currently working in human services, make a list of all

Table 1.   Time management self-assessment

Results		In the next month		In the next week		Tomorrow	
1 (a).	I want my professional activities to result in.....	1.	Ongoing communication with local mental health agencies	1.	Beginning work on finding a speech therapist	1.	Preparing material for coming core meetings
		2.	Better communications with the department	2.	Beginning to write proposal to obtain funding sources for wheelchair	2.	Gathering data for month end reports
1 (b).	My professional activities must result in.....	1.	Finding funding for wheelchair repairs	1.	Completing month end reports	1.	Answering two letters from parents
		2.	Contracting services of a speech therapist	2.	Attending two core meetings	2.	Scheduling meeting on client issues
						3.	Returning phone calls
Process							
2 (a).	I want to spend my professional time.....	1.	Reading related journal articles	1.	Developing plan of in-service training for department	1.	Writing ideas to present to my supervisor
		2.	Attending professional conferences or seminars	2.	Discussing long range plans with my supervisor	2.	Making calls to charitable organization for donations
2 (b).	I must spend my professional time.....	1.	Finding alternative funding sources	1.	Attending meetings	1.	Being in office 8 hours
		2.	Preparing for state inspection	2.	Meeting other requests on time	2.	Responding to phone calls and drop-ins

your nondiscretionary responsibilities, and another list of all the discretionary activities you would like to complete.

    b.   If you are a student, list your school-related discretionary and non-discretionary activities.

5-4.   Still another way to view your professional activities is to divide them into high-payoff activities (HIPOs) and low-payoff activities (LOPOs).

HIPOs are important but they can take time and are often not well defined, such as in the case of long-term planning, building working relationships, long-term development of a new funding source, or establishment of a new treatment program. LOPOs are often specific tasks that are easy to do and that make one feel one has accomplished something. However, they may not make much difference in the long run (Practical Supervision, 1986).

    a.   If you are currently working in human services, list five common professional LOPOs for you and five common HIPOs.

    b.   If you are a student, list five common school-related LOPOs and five common HIPOs for you.

Assessment of Current Time Use

If you want to find out whether you are meeting your goals for use of your professional time, you need to know how you are currently using your time and if you are currently achieving your professional goals. One way to assess your current use of time is by keeping a time log like the one shown in Figure 1.

    Following is an example of a time log for 1 work day for Bill Martinez. Bill is a counselor in a program for unemployed veterans.

Exercises

5-5.   Keep a time log for a week (or for as long as you can, if a week is too long), using the chart shown (see Figure 2). Under "Cues" and "Consequences" include anything you think might be related to how you used your time.

5-6.   Now look at your answers to the chart you completed for exercise 5-2 about how you *want* to spend your time and how you *must* spend your time. Compare those answers to how you really spent your time as shown on your time log. Did you meet your goals?

5-7.   Finally, look at your answers to the chart you completed for exercise 5-2 about what you want to accomplish and what you are required to accomplish in the next week. Compare these answers to what you actually accomplished during the week you completed the time log. Did you meet your goals?

Date	Time	Cues	What I did	Consequences
7/10	8:30	Smell of coffee	Chatted with Jan and Mark	Avoided phone messages
	9:30		Made calls	Got stiff from sitting
	10:45	Heard mail delivery	Got mail, wrote letters	Moved around, felt better
	11:30	Hunger!	Met client for lunch (had appt.)	Felt good: helped client solve a problem
	1:00		Went to staff meeting	Learned about new technique
	2:00–5:00		Conducted one group and two individual sessions	Tired! Two sessions went well, one didn't

Figure 1.   Time Log for Bill Martinez.

Analyzing Time Use Problems

If you answered "No" to either of Exercises 5-6 or 5-7, you are not meeting your time use goals. This means you should be scheduling your time differently at work or at school. There are three general types of time use problems.

In the first type, there are situations that lead you to use time in ways you want to change, or the situation discourages you from spending time the way you want to spend your time. Some typical examples of cues that lead you to time misuse are:

Your best friend at work shares an office with you, so you often turn to him or her to chat about nonwork related activities.

You share an office with someone who procrastinates or gossips often.

An unexpected change in your schedule leaves you with an hour with nothing planned.

Your boss interrupts your work on an important report to give you a new project that has to be done "yesterday."

Your phone rings throughout the day.

The smell of freshly brewed coffee leads you to the break room.

Your office is too hot or too cold.

Date	Time	Cues	What I did	Consequences

Figure 2. Time Log (sample form).

In the second type, you do not have the skills you need to manage certain kinds of time effectively. Examples of skills needed to manage time effectively are:

Ability to chair a meeting in a way that gives everyone the chance to contribute but no one the chance to monopolize
Ability to gracefully end a conversation with someone who wants to keep talking to you
Ability to control phone interruptions
Ability to say "No," when you already have too much to do
Ability to set up a daily 'to do' list and work through it
Ability to set up a useful filing system

In the third type of time use problem, you are either not getting enough rewards for using your time in a way that meets your goals, or you are getting too many rewards for using your time inappropriately. Rewards can keep people from using time well, because one can receive them for time mismanagement. Following are examples of these rewards.

Attention   Some people get attention by playing the martyr and telling others how hard they work ("Oh, how overworked I am"!). Also, many people continue to arrive late for meetings because they get to be the center of attention, particularly if they rush in breathless and apologetically say they were managing a crisis (Scott, 1980).

Power   Most of us have been at meetings wherein one of the people whose presence is needed arrives 15 minutes late. If you need this person's input to arrive at a group decision, showing up late places that person in a powerful position (Scott, 1980).

Avoidance of Tasks   When we procrastinate and put off unpleasant tasks, it is often with the hope that, if we delay long enough, someone else will do our work for us. Also, sometimes we put off boring or unpleasant tasks because it is more fun to "brainstorm" with colleagues (the solution to this is to reward yourself for finishing that boring report by spending time in more enjoyable professional activities) (Scott, 1980).

Resistance to Change   Change is hard for most people. It can be very difficult to give up old, familiar ways of managing time even if new tactics will be more effective (Scott, 1980).

Avoidance of Responsibility   When you hear someone say "Why didn't you remind me those reports were due yesterday"? you are hearing someone who is avoiding taking responsibility for their own actions (Scott, 1980).

Excitement and Stimulation Some people need more excitement in their lives than others. If they have not found functional ways to get that excitement, they may use time mismanagement to get more stimulation. Those individuals who always run in breathlessly at the last minute, or who always meet deadlines with seconds to spare may be filling their personal excitement quota (Scott, 1980).

Exercises

5-8. Use the information you have from exercises 5-1 through 5-7 to decide whether your approach to time management is in need of any improvements. If it is, analyze your current use and decide:
   a. If there are cues for time use you want to change
   b. If there are new time management skills you want to learn
   c. If there are changes you want to make in the consequences you receive for your time use

Design and Use of Time Management Skills

After you have identified your time use goals, identified any ways in which you are not meeting these goals, and identified problems with cues, skills, and/or consequences that may need to be solved, it is time to pick a solution. Following are several typical ways to improve the way you use your time at work. Remember, however, these are techniques that may not work for everyone. Use your creativity to pick time management strategies that will work for you!

CUES FOR TIME MANAGEMENT

Sometimes it is difficult to manage your time effectively because it is not clear what you are supposed to be doing. A common starting place for improving time management is to ask for clarification about your responsibilities, how they differ from other people's responsibilities, and what results you are expected to achieve (Maher & Cook, 1985). If you ask for a specific job description and do not get one, write one and ask for it to be approved by your supervisor.

It is amazing how many people expect to be able to remember all the things they are supposed to do without writing them down. Unless you are the rare individual who has a photographic memory, lists are important time management tools. Most of us are familiar with the daily "to do" list. "To do" lists are often divided into three categories: things to do, calls to make, and people to see. It is also helpful to always have paper and pencil with you at work to make lists of tasks as they occur to you. In the middle of a meeting, for instance, you may suddenly remember that you need to call Ms. Johnson. Or, during a phone conversation you may remember a letter you promised to write for Mr. Martin. If you have something to write with and something to write on, you can capture those tasks on paper.

Another common barrier to effective time management may be found in poor scheduling. If this is a problem for you, consider the calendar you use. As with other techniques, no one calendar works for everyone. Experiment until you find one that is right for you. Then, when you schedule time, be sure that you:

1. Reserve enough time for each activity (including time for travel with some extra for traffic jams and road construction).
2. Match the task to the time of day and your energy level (for example, if you do your best paperwork in the morning, hold all calls between 8 A.M. and 9 A.M.).
3. Match the activity to the people and resources you need to complete the activity (e.g., make sure the people you need to consult on that special project are available at the times you want to consult them).
4. Divide big projects into small manageable steps and set deadlines for completing each step (Maher & Cook, 1985).
5. Finally, do not forget to make appointments with yourself. It is too easy to schedule only meetings and appointments that involve other people; avoid regarding time you need alone to think about projects or to write reports as interruptable and generally less important. In addition, include in your calendar some way to remind yourself of routine responsibilities or follow-up calls you need to complete. This type of reminder is often called a "tickler file."

One of the most important tools used in human services is the telephone. Unfortunately, it is also one of the biggest barriers to effective time management. Sometimes, it is not possible to have calls held or to have them screened routinely. If it is possible, do have calls held if you are in a meeting (including meetings with yourself), and do have calls screened so that you can pull out any notes you need or otherwise prepare for the call. Some people set up regular times they make outgoing and accept incoming calls every day, so that most of their phone work can be done in one time period (Maher & Cook, 1985). If your organization will not allow you to limit incoming calls, you can still provide cues for people to call at certain times. For instance, you might tell callers: "The best time to reach me is before noon," or: "I'm usually easier to reach if you call on Monday, Wednesday, or Thursday." Also, if you are interrupted by a call while you are in the middle of a project, you can say something like: "I'm in the middle of something else right now. May I get back to you in an hour"? One indispensable aid to effective use of the phone is a list of frequently used phone numbers. Some people prefer to use address books, others choose files of business cards or some other system. Again, use whatever works for you.

Another obstacle to efficient time management can be your filing system. No one filing system works for everyone. Consider what papers you will need often and set up a system that makes it easy for you to find and retrieve those papers.

Waiting is something we all do, often unexpectedly. We wait for meetings to start, for cars to be repaired, for appointments with health care providers. Sometimes it is possible to call ahead and find out whether there will be a wait. More often, waits cannot be predicted. Waiting time can be productive time if you always have short tasks or reading with you. Some of the authors' most productive professional time has been spent in car repair shop waiting rooms, because no one can call us there!

Time Management Skills

Managing Time Alone   One of the hardest skills to learn can be doing just one thing at a time. Often, since there is always too much to do in human services, as you work on one task three others occur to you that are also important. A useful way to cope effectively when this happens is to make a note of the other tasks, but not to interrupt your original work to do them (Maher & Cook, 1985). Another common problem is having many different things to do and not being able to decide where to begin. A possible solution to this problem is to give every job a due date, so that you can pick what to do next depending on when you want to have it done. A deadline does not have to be imposed on you from the outside: it can be your decision about when you want to complete a job. Another approach some people find useful is to do part of one project, then move on to part of another project, and so on. This tactic increases variety, but may not be for you if you like to concentrate on one project for an extended period of time.

Another useful approach to managing the time you work alone is to group similar tasks together. For instance, you might make all the phone calls on your to do list in 1 hour, deal with all your correspondence in 1 half-hour, and so on. When you schedule a large block of time to do desk work, it helps to get up and walk around every so often.

No one can concentrate on one task indefinitely, so it helps to give yourself a break and some variety.

Managing Time in Meetings Most meetings can be improved by having time limits, having set agenda, by including only necessary people, and beginning and ending promptly. If you are not clear about the purpose of a meeting, ask! If you are not clear about what you are expected to contribute, ask! If you are chairing a meeting, it is your responsibility to clarify the purpose of the meeting and the contributions expected from all participants. And it is your responsibility to begin and end the meeting on time.

Managing Interruptions It is not always possible to avoid interruptions by having calls held or by closing your office door. In that case, skills at managing interruptions become important. Most people are receptive if you diplomatically tell them you are in the middle of a project and then ask them when you can get back to them. This may not, however, be a comfortable tactic if the person interrupting you is your supervisor. An interruption from a supervisor can often be handled effectively with a response such as: "I'm about halfway done with the report you asked me to complete by this afternoon. Would you prefer that I put the report on hold for the moment, or shall I get back to you on this new issue later"? This approach lets your supervisor know what you are doing and takes the choice about whether to continue the interruption out of your hands.

Learning To Say "No" The better you are at your job, the more likely people are to ask you to do additional work. In addition, human service agencies never have enough money, so there is always more work to do than there are people to do it. It is helpful to remember that if you try to do too much, you will not do anything very well. One graceful way to say "No" to additional work is to explain: "I'm very flattered that you asked, but I'm so busy already that if I said yes I would not be able to do it as well as both of us would want the job done."

Learning To Do It Anyway Sometimes a job has to be done right away and you do not want to do it right away. The only solution, if there is no escape, is to grit your teeth and do it anyway.

REWARDING YOURSELF FOR EFFECTIVE TIME MANAGEMENT

A common trap that causes numerous time management problems is to say: "I'll do this task that I enjoy first and save the unpleasant one for later." This approach sets you up for failure, because it is designed to punish you (by having you do a job you do not enjoy) for doing some-

thing you find pleasant. A more successful strategy is to give yourself
the opportunity to do something you like as a reward for completing
an unpleasant chore. For instance, you might reward yourself for making a difficult phone call by having a brainstorming session with a favorite co-worker.

Another way to reward yourself for using time effectively is to put
up a chart, graph, or sign in your office that shows how much you have
accomplished. You can post any type of information you choose: number of calls made, number of reports completed, and amount of time
spent providing direct service are examples of information human service professionals have posted.

Exercises
5-9.   Design a time management improvement plan for yourself and use it for
       a week.

Evaluating Time Use Interventions
No time management tactic is worth using unless it helps you achieve
your goals. Once you have started using a new approach to some part
of time management, you will first need to use it long enough to give it
a fair trial. Then it is time to decide whether your new approach is a
success. Good questions to ask as you decide are:

Did you meet your goal?
If you have met your goal, was your new tactic responsible for your
      success?
Were there any unintended side effects resulting from your new tactic?
How do you feel about what you have done and the results you have
      achieved? (adapted from Maher & Cook, 1985)

If you decide your tactic is a success, all you have to do is to keep
using it. If it is not successful, drop it and try a different approach.

Exercises
5-10. Evaluate the time management improvement plan you designed for
       Exercise 5-9.
5-11. Use your time management skills to remind yourself to come back to
       this exercise 1 month after you finish this chapter. When that time
       comes, go back to Exercise 5-1 and answer it again. Have your an-
       swers changed at all during the month? Have your time management
       skills improved?
5-12. Pick a friend or colleague who seems to get a lot done and shadow that
       person for a day.

CHAPTER 6

COMMUNICATION

OR

Did You Say What I Heard?

OBJECTIVES

To be able to:

1. Describe guidelines for effective communication and learn how to use them.
2. Develop a plan for working with difficult persons.

The world runs on communication. Life as we know it simply would not exist if we could not communicate with one another.

> " . . . when the use of language results, as it so often does, in
> the creation or aggravation of disagreements and conflict,
> there is something linguistically wrong with the speaker, the
> listener, or both."
>
> (Hayakawa, 1964, p. 18)

Communication is perhaps more important in human services than in other human endeavors, for all our professional relationships are based on communication. Everyday life is also extraordinarily complex, with endless possibilities for effective or ineffective communication. This chapter is designed to provide the reader with an overview of basic guidelines for effective communication and for working with difficult people. While the strategies described in the chapter are useful both with professionals and with consumers of services, the authors' focus is on communication with colleagues. Communication with service consumers is obviously of great importance; for this reason, human services training programs focus more on this than on communication with colleagues. Hence, this section focuses on communication with co-workers.

Guidelines for Effective Communication

> "The tongue is the most
> mobile structure of the human body."
>
> (Wendell Johnson)

Listen Carefully This is the most repeated and most broken rule for good communication. Careful, active listening requires all of one's attention. This includes attention to verbal and nonverbal cues. Active listening is very different from the kind of listening most of us do in ordinary conversation, when we may daydream and let our minds wander. The most common obstacle to careful listening is failure to pay attention completely. Too often in conversation, we are not really paying attention: we are merely waiting until it is our turn to talk and planning our responses, or we are daydreaming.

Have you ever been talking with someone and realized that what you heard is not what they said? Here is an example of this type of failure in listening skills: your supervisor says she wants the proposal you are working on completed by the end of the week, and that she wants to be kept informed of your progress. You start thinking about what you need to do to finish in time, and do not pay careful attention to the rest of her comments. The next day she comes in to your office at 11:00, irate because you did not follow her instruction to fill her in by 9:00 each morning!

There are two tactics that will help prevent misunderstanding what has been said to you. One tactic is *paraphrasing* (Giampa, Walker-Burt, & Lamb, 1984). When you paraphrase, you test how well you understood what you heard by trying to put the other person's ideas in your own words. For instance, suppose Mark Ryan, one of your colleagues, says to you: "Sandra is so flaky, I can't count on her for anything." Sandra is another one of your colleagues. This is a rather general statement that could refer to any number of problems. To find out whether you and your colleague mean the same thing when you refer to Sandra's flakiness, you might ask: "Do you mean that she is almost always late to meetings"? If your colleague replies "Yes," then your paraphrase has helped you find out that you heard what she said correctly. Suppose your colleague's reply is: "No, she's usually on time for meetings, but very often she doesn't seem well-prepared for them. I don't think she does her homework." This not only tells you your first interpretation was incorrect, it tells you specifically what your colleague meant. Now, suppose your colleague replies: "No, she's usually on time. She's just flaky, you know what I mean." The odds are good at this point that *you do not know what he means.* To find out, you might try asking a question such as: "Well, no, I don't know. Can you give me an example of something she's done recently that you feel is flaky"?

Another useful tactic for the active listener is *perception checking* (Giampa et al., 1984). Perception checking is usually used to find out if the other person is feeling what you think the person is feeling. For instance, you might say: "I get the feeling that you're angry with me right now. Is that true"? Or: "It sounds to me like you're pretty unhappy with the way things are. Is that right"? Of course, if you ask questions such as these you must be willing to hear the answers. If you ask if a person is angry, the response may be: "You bet I'm angry, you so-and-so, and here's why . . ." In the author's opinion, it is better to know what is going on than to ignore subtle signals or misread a situation completely. Further, it is most helpful to check your perceptions as soon as possible after you identify the need to do so. If you wait to check and act on an incorrect perception in the meantime, you may create an unnecessary problem.

Attend to Nonverbal as well as Verbal Communication The following is a partial list of body parts or movements that are used in communication: eyes, hands, handshake, stance, walk, tone of voice, head, face, smile, posture, use of touch, nervous mannerisms such as foot swinging or tapping a pencil, vocal intensity, and vocal volume (Warschaw, 1980). There are books available that claim to tell you what various nonverbal forms of communication mean. Beware of them! Interpretations of nonverbal signals are culturally based (Warschaw, 1980). Thus, the same signal can have two completely different meanings in two different cultures. There are cultures, for instance, where shaking the head up and down means "No," a signal likely to confuse someone from the United States where the same signal means "Yes." Similarly, signals can also have different meanings in different parts of a single country. Another caution is to avoid attributing too much meaning to certain nonverbal behavior. For instance, a person's fidgeting may mean that person is uncomfortable with what you are saying, or it could just as easily mean the available seating is physically uncomfortable, the meeting has lasted too long, or the individual has a medical condition of which tremor or shakiness is a symptom. Some of us are less able to sit still for long meetings than others.

It is important to be aware of the nonverbal signals you are giving as well as those you are receiving. For instance, do you look down at papers on the table when you are uninterested or uncomfortable with what the speaker has to say? Do you avoid eye contact with someone who is expressing anger with you? Avoiding eye contact can be a mistake, for doing so may mute particularly angry or volatile responses. Eye contact may be difficult to provide in these instances, however, for our first impulse is usually not to look at someone who is yelling at us. Do you turn away when you disagree with a speaker? When you are physically uncomfortable, can the ways you show that discomfort be misread as lack of attention or agreement?

Be Sensitive to the Emotional Content of Language Two words with essentially the same dictionary meaning can have vastly different emotional content. Thus, you can create or diffuse emotional situations through the use of language, and you can identify the emotional tone set by others by attending to the emotional content of their language. For instance, consider the following descriptions given by two counselors regarding a client whom they have just seen jointly:

Stan: "Boy, was that last fellow defensive! Uptight and not willing to admit to half the problems in his life. He's going to be difficult to counsel effectively."

Marcia: "We have very different perceptions of our client, Stan. He struck me as reserved, and very clear about what he wanted to discuss and what he did not want to discuss. I think he's set some well-defined limits that I found very reasonable."

Both counselors agreed that the man they saw held some of his emotions back, but they labeled and evaluated that action very differently. The first counselor used the negatively weighted words "uptight" and "defensive," while the second counselor described the same approach as "reserved."

Exercises

6-1. For the next three meetings or classes you attend, pay careful attention to, and make notes concerning, the nonverbal signals given by others and by you. Also note whether the people you observe are responding primarily to verbal or nonverbal signals when the two are not conveying the same message.

6-2. Categorize each word listed below in terms of its emotional value for you. Indicate whether you feel each to be positive, negative, or neutral.

Conservative	Masculine
Liberal	Feminine
Sensitive	Discreet
Defensive	Private

Cheerful	Depressed
Needy	Manipulative
Strong	

6-3. For one day, carry a file card or piece of paper and pencil with you all day and list every word you hear to which you have a strong emotional reaction, whether it is positive or negative.

Remember the Difference between Language and Reality

"A map is not the territory it stands for; words are not things. A map does not represent all of a territory; words never say all about anything.

The meanings of words are not in the words; they are in us. Beware of definitions, which are words about words. Think with examples rather than definitions whenever possible."

(Hayakawa, 1964, p. 314–315)

Many of the words we use to describe how people act are summary words: they are a personal shorthand for a number of discrete behaviors. The previous example using the word "flaky" illustrates use of such a summary word. Probably the most common and misused summary word the authors know is "inappropriate." *Never,* when told someone is acting in a way that is "inappropriate," assume you know specifically what the speaker means! We have heard "inappropriate" to mean everything from: "She wears pants and I think she should be wearing a skirt," to: "He exposes his genitals in public," with a host of other interpretations in between. That is why Hayakawa's recommendation to think with examples is so important. If you think with examples and use paraphrasing, your ability to understand what other speakers are saying will be much greater than if you simply assume you know what others are talking about.

Beware of Jargon Jargon is generally vague and inexact; for this reason, it inevitably makes communication less effective. Occasionally, human services workers use jargon or abbreviations, and when they do, they often are so accustomed to these terms that they forget others do not understand. Sometimes we use jargon to control a situation by keeping others ignorant. If a colleague with whom you are speaking sprinkles conversations with jargon which you do not understand, *ask* what the speaker means. To reduce your own use of jargon, you may want to keep a list of acronyms and terms to avoid so that people who use your services and/or colleagues in other agencies will know what you are talking about. Reducing one's use of jargon will be useful because many service consumers may feel too intimidated to ask for clarification of such terms.

Jargon that interferes with communication is not limited to human services. When the authors first moved to Denver, they made use of a city map to figure out how to get around. On the map, there were two major interstate highways, I-25 going North and South and I-70 going East and West. However, the newscasters on local radio stations kept referring to traffic conditions on the "Valley Highway." We could not find the Valley Highway on the map. It took several months before we figured out that the Valley Highway was the same as I-25!

If You Have Just Reached an Important Agreement, Write It Down! Putting an important agreement in writing serves two purposes. First, it serves as a final check to make sure everyone understood what was discussed and agrees to the same thing. This prevents misunderstandings. For example, in a meeting with Mr. Smith from Generic Services Inc., Mr. Smith says: "Joe Taylor needs social skills training." You say: "Yes, I agree." At the end of your meeting, some 30 minutes later, Mr. Smith says: "Now, you're going to provide Mr. Taylor with social skills training and I'll provide the other services we've discussed." Your response clarifies what was actually agreed upon: "No, I didn't agree to provide that service; I just agreed it was needed."

The second advantage of putting agreements in writing is that it prevents faulty memory from interfering with the implementation of the agreement at a later date. Most of us have been at parties where we have played "Telephone." In this game, one person whispers a statement to a second person, who then whispers it to a third person, and so on, until everyone in the room has heard it. The final person to hear the message repeats it out loud. Invariably, what the final person says and what the first person said are very different.

Say Only What You Are Willing to Have Repeated If you have just finished a frustrating meeting with someone from another agency, resist the urge to go to the staff lounge and announce: "That so-and-so from that agency is a real jerk"! Such an announcement should be avoided because chances are good you will have future contact with "that so-and-so." Chances are also good that someone who hears you will repeat your comment to an employee of the agency across the street, who will repeat it to the subject of your comment. Also, people who hear you say something negative about an absent colleague will wonder what you say about them when they are not around. In addition to being unsafe, nasty remarks about colleagues are also very unprofessional and are unlikely to improve anyone's impression of you.

Use Feedback Effectively

> " Giving feedback is reporting one's
> observations of and reactions to another's behavior."
>
> (Giampa et al., 1984, p.17)

Effective feedback has several characteristics:

1. **It is proactive.** It focuses on what you want the person *to do,* not on what you want the person to stop doing. Taking a proactive approach improves the likelihood of a positive future relationship with the person receiving feedback. It also improves the likelihood that the person receiving feedback will change or consider changing in the manner you suggest. Here are two examples of proactive feedback:

    "Sandie, I really appreciate the way you helped me with the Evans family this morning: Your knowledge of a different solution helped everyone get what they wanted. I hope you'll let me call on you for that kind of help again."

    "Mary, I appreciate your willingness to chair the meeting this morning. However, when you said, 'We all know what the problem is, let's find a solution,' I felt cut off because I'm not sure I agree with your identification of the problem. When this sort of thing comes up in the future, could you ask for other people's views on the nature of the problem before moving on"?

    The first example described to the person receiving feedback what she had done that the speaker wanted her to keep doing. The second example started with a positive statement and then described to Mary what the speaker wanted her to do differently.

2. **It is specific.** It tells the person what was done well and/or what needs to change.

3. **It separates what the person did from its emotional effect on you.** Instead of saying: "You made me very angry this morning," say: "When you told me not to get involved in your project, I felt very angry."

4. **It is about behavior or conditions the listener is able to change.** There is no point in giving corrective feedback about a rule that was made by Congress, and that the listener is responsible for implementing but cannot change.

5. **It is well-timed.** On one hand, feedback that is given as soon as possible after the incident occurs makes it easy for the listener to remember the events to which the speaker is referring. On the

other hand, if you have just had a very emotionally charged meeting, you may want to wait until everyone has a chance to calm down before offering any feedback.

6. **It includes a clarity check.** When you give well thought out feedback, you will want to make sure that the listener hears what you said. One way to accomplish this goal is to, as diplomatically as possible, ask the listener to paraphrase what she or he has heard you say.

(adapted from Giampa et al., 1984)

It is often difficult to give effective feedback, especially corrective feedback. One way to make giving feedback easier is to start small; another way is to practice giving purely positive feedback first, so that one can become comfortable with it. Then, start giving small corrections to nonthreatening people and build up gradually.

Face Your Fears Sometimes we do not communicate clearly because we are afraid of what we imagine to be the possible results. Some common fears are: fear of failing to meet expectations, fear of offending or hurting others, fear of rejection, fear of being wrong, or fear of being unable to express oneself accurately. In some situations, those fears may be realistic, in other situations, they may not. Either way, communicating poorly will not improve relationships. It may delay whatever consequences, good or bad, there will be from what you need to communicate. However, the delay will probably cause new problems, as people become frustrated when they cannot understand what someone else is saying.

Ask for Help No one has perfect communication skills. Further, other people may be reluctant to give you feedback about your communication skills. It helps to be willing to ask for feedback or to ask for specific advice on how to improve your skills. For instance, at the end of a difficult meeting, you might approach someone who also attended the meeting and whose judgment you trust and ask if your points came across clearly.

Much human services work requires interaction with a variety of professions and people. If you are unsure about how to communicate effectively with members of another profession, ask them for assistance! One useful approach is to ask: "What questions should I be asking you"? (Warschaw, 1980). Another is to ask what information the person would find helpful to receive from you.

A good rule of thumb to remember about asking for help is that it is usually acceptable to make a mistake once, but it is not acceptable to keep making the same mistake. That is why it is better to ask for help than to flounder.

Exercises

6-4. For one day, pay careful attention to how people communicate at work and/or at school. Try to identify at least one example of each of the following:

Careful listening:
Attention to nonverbal cues
Sensitivity to emotional content
Recognition of the difference between language and reality
Effective use of feedback

Poor listening:
Failure to attend to nonverbal cues
Insensitivity to emotional content
Failure to recognize the difference between language and reality
Jargon that obscures meaning
Gossip
Ineffective use of feedback
Defensiveness

6-5. For each of the examples of poor listening you found in exercise 6-4, describe how the communicator could have made the communication more effective.

6-6. a. List the 10 jargon words or phrases most frequently used at your agency or office.
b. Translate each of those words or phrases into everyday language that will be easily understood by an individual totally unfamiliar with the field of human services.

WORKING WITH DIFFICULT PEOPLE

"The leverage is in the interaction."

(Bramson, 1981, p. 143)

This last part of the chapter concerns the process of interacting with people whose actions you regularly find frustrating. Examples of difficult behavior include: the colleague who smiles and nods when you ask him to do something, and then does not do it, the supervisor who starts yelling at you when you indicate that what she has just said is unclear, or your counterpart at another agency who does not return your calls. These are people with whom it is difficult to work. Their behavior may trigger strong emotional reactions in you, reactions that make it hard to behave calmly and proactively. There are three ways you can respond to people who act in problematic ways: 1) you can try to change their behavior, which is likely to be a slow process with no guarantee of success, 2) you can give in, or 3) you can cope. Coping involves contending with people on equal terms, and is a way to establish a balance of power in a relationship (Bramson, 1981). People you find difficult to work with generally have power over you; coping is a way to establish an equal balance of power in the relationship so that you can both get on with business (Bramson, 1981).

Suppose you work with someone you find difficult. You are constantly exasperated and frustrated by interactions with this person, and, as a result, are unable to complete an important part of your job. You find yourself reacting to this person, rather than planning how to handle difficult situations in advance. Simply reacting will not help you in the long run, as it places the difficult person in control. The following steps will help you to proactively cope with the problem.

1. Ask yourself whether the problem is the person or the current situation. If the problem is not one you typically have with this person, you may just want to sit down with him or her and ask what is happening. If the problem is a continual one, move on to step (2).
2. Get some distance from the situation. Choose a time and a place that remove you enough so that you can consider the problem calmly. For instance, if your problem is with the person in the office next to yours, you may want to leave your office and find a quiet place farther away.
3. Describe in detail, preferably in writing, the behavior of the person you find difficult. For example, the following is a description by Sam of a colleague who is a complainer. Every time Sam says more than "hello" to him, the colleague has something to complain about. Some of the things the colleague has said recently are:

    "Have you heard the latest? There's another form to fill out before we can help people."

    "This coffee is terrible. Someone must be dumping motor oil in it."

    "That client is just going to take our money and gamble it away, and there isn't a thing we can do about it."

    "The boss is at it again. Now she wants us to have a goal planning session. What a waste of time"!
4. Describe what you did when faced with the behaviors you just listed. Describe your own actions in as much detail as possible. Here are some of Sam's sample responses to the complaints listed above:

"I didn't think it was so bad."

"Yes, it is."

"Well, we don't have any rules about how they spend the money."

"It's a nice break in the routine."

5. Review the interactions you described, and answer these questions:

   a. What did you want to accomplish during those interactions? Sam wants to avoid unpleasantness and to stop hearing further complaints.

   b. What did you do that seemed to work (that is, what did you do to make progress toward accomplishing your goals)? Sam did avoid further unpleasantness in each individual interaction, but he was not successful at ending the other person's complaining.

   c. What did you do that did not seem to work?

6. Given your answers to (5), describe what you need to do to more effectively cope with your problem person. Answer these questions:

   a. What skills do I need to use that I already have? Sam clearly is able to stay calm and pleasant in response to the complaints, and to identify the positive aspects of unpleasant situations.

   b. What skills do I need to learn in order to cope with this problem? Sam clearly needs to learn skills that will stop the complaining permanently. According to Bramson (1981), these are: listen attentively to the complaint; check your perception of how the person feels by paraphrasing; do not agree or apologize, even if the complaint is legitimate. Additionally, state the facts and acknowledge them, but do not comment; try to move to a problem-solving mode; if all else fails, ask how the complainer wants the conversation to end.

7. Use your answers to (6) to write an action plan that specifies what you will do and when.

8. Set a time to review your progress toward an effective coping strategy. When you conduct your review, decide whether your plan is working. If not, revise it.

(*Note.* Adapted from *Coping with Difficult People* by Robert Bramson. Copyright © 1981 by Robert M. Bramson. Reprinted by permission of Doubleday, a division of Bantam, Doubleday, Dell Publishing Group, Inc.)

COPING STRATEGY IN ACTION

Ethel is a "sniper." Whenever Amanda makes a suggestion at a meeting, Ethel has a comment such as: "There goes our college graduate again, being high and mighty and trying to improve us." These comments are always made with a smile and a pleasant tone of voice, so that they are not openly hostile. Ethel is also a master of snide remarks about the boss whenever he is not present. Recent examples include: "Well, he certainly was pleasant today in staff meeting—I wonder what extra work he's dreaming up for us." When Amanda presented a new approach to delivering one type of service, Ethel said: "There goes Amanda, playing up to the boss again."

Here is how Amanda developed a coping plan for working with Ethel:

1. Is this a consistent problem? Yes, it is. Ethel snipes all the time.
2. I need some distance. Amanda finds an empty conference room and puts a "Meeting in Progress—Do Not Disturb" sign on the door.
3. Describe the behavior. Amanda generates the descriptions given above.
4. Describe your reactions. When Ethel said: "There goes our college graduate again" I turned red, muttered something about "just trying to contribute to the team" and shut up. When Ethel made the crack about playing up to the boss, I became angry but did not say anything, and soon after left for the women's restroom to regain control of my temper.
5. What did I want to accomplish? I wanted to control my temper and shut her up. I did manage to control my temper, except for turning red, but she never shuts up. Failure to respond emotionally seems to help me gain control, but it doesn't prevent future attacks.
6. Clearly I need to continue to control my emotions while learning a way to prevent ongoing attacks. I think I need to be more direct with Ethel.
7. Here is my plan. The next time she snipes at me in a staff meeting, I'm going to confront her directly with something like: "Ethel, that sounds like you're making fun of me. Is that what you mean to do"? She will probably deny that she is making fun, but that's okay. The other thing she might do is tell me that what I'm suggesting is all wrong and why. If she does that, I'll try to find out what everyone else thinks, for example by asking: "Anyone else agree with that point of view"? If others agree there is a problem with my idea, I'll

suggest we try to solve it. It's okay for her to criticize my ideas as long as the criticism is open and can be discussed: it's not okay for her to snipe at me. I suppose one other way she could react is to agree that she is making fun of me. If she does, I'll tell her that, like most people, I don't like being made fun of, and ask if she's willing to stop. If she admits publicly to making fun of me, I think it's okay to put her on the spot.

My biggest problem with this plan will be staying calm, because Ethel makes me see red when she snipes. I'll try to take a slow, deep breath before I make any response to her sniping.

8. I'll review the situation in 3 weeks and decide whether I've made any progress.

This strategy often helps, but it does not lead to success every time you use it. Sometimes your best efforts to cope fail. Then it is time to remember that you always have a choice about whether you continue to stay in contact with a person whose behavior is consistently difficult (Bramson, 1981). This is not an easy choice, particularly if your difficult person is your supervisor and your choice is to find another job. However, choosing to withdraw from contact is always your final option.

" Cherish an awareness that coping with Difficult
People is *never* easy and hardly ever fun. If you
know what you're doing, you ought to feel uneasy.
Acknowledgment of fear is the first step toward moving
beyond it. "

(Bramson, 1981, p. 175)

Exercises

6-7. Pick one difficult person you must interact with regularly at work or at school. Use the eight steps above to develop a plan for coping with that person.

CHAPTER 7

PROFESSIONAL DEVELOPMENT

OR

Find Your Job and Love It

OBJECTIVES

To be able to:

1. Describe the characteristics of the ideal job for you.
2. Prepare the materials needed to apply for a position.
3. Prepare for a professional interview.
4. Develop formal and informal professional development opportunities.

"It is possible to work 10 years and have either
10 years of experience or 1 year of experience 10 times.**"**

Anonymous

The person who gets 10 years of experience in 10 years has never stopped learning. The person who has had 1 year of experience 10 times learned to do things in a certain way the first year on the job and continued to do them the same way for the next 9 years. This chapter is about becoming the professional who never stops learning and improving his or her professional skills.

There are three main ways to further your professional development. One is to enter a degree program in a community college, undergraduate college or university, or graduate school program. The second way to further your professional development is to find a job in your field that will give you the opportunity to learn and grow. Finally, you may choose to develop your knowledge and skills through methods that do not involve a degree program. These include: specialized training programs, certificate programs, seminars, or nondegree or noncredit college courses. Most people choose some combination of degree programs, on-the-job training, and/or specialized training during their careers. The authors' focus is on helping the reader to find a job in which the reader is able to grow. Additionally, nondegree based professional development will be discussed.

Finding a Job

Before you begin looking for work, you need to answer a few basic questions. These include:

1. What type of work do you want to do? Be specific about the types of activities in which you are interested, the characteristics of the consumers you wish to serve, and what you want to accomplish.
2. Under what conditions are you willing to work? Where are you willing to live? Are you willing to be a live-in staff member? Are you willing to move geographically? What hours are you willing to work?
3. What salary and benefits do you expect to receive? How much will you settle for? Which benefits are most important?

Your Resumé

There are many approaches to putting together a professional resumé. The design you choose is probably less important than the information you include. Following is a list of information to include on your resumé:

Employment History Include exact dates of all relevant positions, job titles, employer names, and brief descriptions of your responsibilities. Do not give only the year you held a previous job, because the employer cannot tell whether you held the job for one day or the entire year. Instead, use a phrase such as "From 1/87 through 8/88."

Educational History Include dates of all degrees, dates of attendance in programs where you have not completed a degree, and the name of the educational institution. Also include any other specialized or technical training (e.g., psychiatric technician) training that may be of interest to an employer. For instance, list a 2-month undergraduate internship at a community mental health center if you are applying for a position in a treatment program for persons with chronic mental illnesses.

Other Relevant Information Please note our emphasis on the word "relevant." Volunteer work is relevant if you acquired or refined a job-related skill. Volunteer experience can also tell the employer about characteristics such as commitment and reliability. Some employers find information about special interests, activities, and awards helpful in giving them a feel for the person.

Information to Omit from Your Resumé Do not include: your age, sex, height, weight, religion, marital status, ethnicity, state of health, ages and names of children, hobbies, or any other personal information in your resumé. If personal information is relevant to the job, the employer will ask for it. If it is not relevant to the job, the information is probably illegal for the employer to solicit. Further, it is worth remembering that an employer who will hire you on the basis of your personal characteristics might also fire you on the same basis.

Finally, the authors recommend strongly against heading your resumé with a career objective or goal (some career counselors disagree with us on this point). Most of the objectives we have seen are either so broad as to be meaningless or so specific that they do not apply to most positions. Broad career goals do not, in our opinion, improve the likelihood that the employer will want to interview you. We assume you want "to serve people and to maximize your professional growth," so why bother to state the obvious?

Occasionally, a career objective is stated specifically. The problem with concrete objectives is that job applicants tend to misuse them. If you have a concrete objective on your resumé, you should use that version of your resumé to apply *only* for positions that will help you to achieve that objective; similarly, you should have different versions of your resumé available for different types of positions. If you apply for a job that does not fit with your career objective, the employer is justified in wondering how serious you are about the position.

One possible resumé format is shown in Figure 1.

Exercises

7-1. If you do not have a resumé, write one. If you do have a resumé, review it and make any needed revisions to bring it up to date.

LETTERS OF APPLICATION

The importance of the letter of application cannot be overstated. The letter of application is your first contact with a possible employer and includes your resumé. There are a variety of guides to writing good letters you can use if you are not sure of your ability to put together a

Rebecca J. Allen

Office: 727 E. Third   Home: 1433 N.
   Anywhere, ZZ   Boulevard
   11111   Anywhere, ZZ
   (000) XXX-XXXX   11112
               (000) XXX-XXXX

PROFESSIONAL EXPERIENCE

FAMILY SERVICES
727 E. Third
Anywhere, ZZ 11111

7/86–present Position: Program Supervisor
     Responsibilities: Include all those listed below as well as supervising six program managers and representing the agency at intake meetings

9/84–6/86 Position: Program Manager
     Responsibilities: Maintain a caseload of 14 children in 10 foster homes; provide bimonthly home visits to monitor child needs and progress; train foster parents in treatment implementation; maintain regular documentation; arrange for necessary medical services; coordinate services with schools, social services, and social security; crisis resolution as needed.

Child Treatment Services
1500 South Hill Street
Somewhere, BB 99999

6/83–8/84 Position: Treatment Staff
     Responsibilities: Implementation of treatment plans for six children ages 7–10 in residential treatment facility. Work closely with other team members, including agency social worker, families of children in treatment, and consulting psychologist.

EDUCATIONAL EXPERIENCE

9/83–5/84 State University
     Bachelor of Social Work, May, 1984

9/80–8/83 City State College

various times I have attended training seminars on: goal planning in child services, legal issues, and professional communication.

(continued

PROFESSIONAL ORGANIZATIONS

My State Association of Child Social Workers   full member
membership
chairperson
7/87–present

PROFESSIONAL REFERENCES

John Green, Executive Director
Family Services
Anywhere, ZZ
(000) XXX-XXXX

Samuel Marshall, Ph.D.
Department of Social Work
University of My State
Anywhere, ZZ
(000) XXX-XXXX

Margaret Smith, Treatment Supervisor
Child Treatment Services
Anywhere, ZZ
(000) XXX-XXXX

Figure 1. Resumé: Rebecca J. Allen.

good letter. Your public library is a good place to find helpful guides, or the career development department of your local bookstore. Then, if you want to make a good first impression:

1. Type your letters! It is amazing how many people apply for professional positions with handwritten notes. If you do not have a typewriter, borrow or rent one, or pay to have your letters typed. Public libraries often have typewriters available for patrons.
2. Check your spelling. Better yet, if you are not a good speller, have someone else who is a good speller check it for you.
3. If you make mistakes, the best way to correct them is to retype the entire letter. If you must use correction fluid, make sure it is the same color as the paper you are using.
4. Use a copy machine that will give you clean copies of your resumé that are as clear as the original.
5. Make an effort to obtain the full name of the agency director or personnel director to whom your letter will be addressed.
6. Avoid sending obvious copies (rather than originals) of your letter

of application. If you are using a word processor, use letter quality print and be sure each letter is personally addressed to its recipient. It is a major faux pas to type a letter and write the recipient's name in by hand. No one will take you seriously if it is obvious that you have sent out a bulk mailing of letters and resumés.

Exercises

7-2. Imagine finding an ad for the position of your dreams. Write a letter of application designed to convince the reader that you are the best person to interview for the position. You may use only the qualifications and experience you actually have. A sample is shown in Figure 2.

YOUR REFERENCES

Your resumé should list names, addresses, and telephone numbers for at least three references, or it should indicate that references are available upon request. If you do not list references on your resumé, have a typed list of them ready to give to a prospective employer when you go for an interview. Your first choice for references should be supervisors or other authorities who have been in a position to observe your skills and abilities. Former professors or colleagues may also be appropriate. Individuals who can attest to your character but not to your professional skills cannot hurt, but they may not help much. You may choose not to list your current or immediate past supervisor because you expect that person to give you a negative reference. If so, you may be asked by an interviewer why you omitted that person's name from the list. It is best to be honest without going into great detail if you are asked this question. For instance, you might say: "I felt Ms. Morrison would not describe my skills as favorably as the people I did list because we had several disagreements about appropriate treatment for my clients."

The Interview

Preparing for the Interview   You will create an excellent first impression in an interview if you do some homework about the agency before you go. Find out about it by asking for materials such as brochures, asking other agencies, and asking friends in human services. If you walk into the interview with some knowledge of the agency's goals and programs, you have demonstrated your interest in the position to the interviewer.

1234 Main Street
Anytown, USA 99999
September 17, 1988

Dorothy Sampson, Executive Director
Main Street Placement Agency
555 Central Avenue
Anytown, USA 99999

Dear Ms. Sampson;

I am writing to apply for the Job Placement Specialist position you advertised in the Metro Times yesterday.

I believe you will find me well-qualified for the position. I have recently completed my B.S. in Vocational Rehabilitation and have three years of direct experience working as a job placement specialist.

Enclosed is a copy of my resumé. I look forward to hearing from you at your earliest convenience. I can be reached at work during weekdays, XXX-XXXX, and at home at other times, XXX-XXXX.

Sincerely,

Martin J. Duran

Figure 2.   Cover letter.

The employer's first impression of you is based on your letter of application and your resumé. The first impression you create at the interview is equally important. Your task is to convince the employer that you are serious about the position. There are two easy ways to do this. One is to *arrive on time*. Few mistakes are as deadly as arriving late for an interview. No one will ever fault you for being 15 minutes early, so plan plenty of time to cope with unexpected traffic delays or late buses. Also, if you are a few minutes early, you will have time to catch your breath and become more comfortable before the interview begins. The second easy way to create a good impression is to *dress up for the interview*. While dress standards vary in different parts of the country, a coat and tie for men and a skirt or dressy slacks for women are usually appropriate. Make-up and cologne, if used, should be subdued. In general, one should plan to dress more formally for the interview than one would for the job.

The Interview   Take the time to answer questions thoughtfully and carefully. Make eye contact with the interviewer regularly and offer a firm handshake when you introduce yourself. Listen carefully to the interviewer's name and title and ask for them again if needed. Then, call the interviewer by her or his last name unless invited to do otherwise (i.e., Ms., Mr., or Dr. Whatever). It is always better to be too formal than to be too informal. If you are being interviewed by two or more people, be equally polite and formal with all of them. Never make assumptions about who will make the hiring decision. One common mistake the authors have observed is made when a job applicant is formal toward the male interviewer but informal and familiar with the female member of the team, who happens to be the boss!

Perhaps the two most important things you have to tell an employer in an interview are: 1) why you want that particular job, and 2) what skills and abilities you have that will be beneficial to the agency. The interviewer is interested in what you have to offer the organization, so you need to tell that person what you have to offer before there is any mention of what the organization has to offer you. Your first response to: "Why are you interested in this position"? should *not* be: "I am starting back to school and the hours fit well with my class schedule," or: "I need a change," or: "The salary is attractive." That may well be true, but most employers will not be pleased if it is your primary motive for wanting the job. A better answer would be: "Your program has a reputation for providing good services for people and good working conditions for staff. I think I can make a contribution here and can learn from you."

You should be prepared to answer questions about why you want to leave your current position, and what you see as your professional strengths and weaknesses. Many employers in human services will ask you if you are willing to make a commitment to the position of at least a year. You may also be asked if you are willing to work evenings or weekends, or if you would work in a setting that bans smoking (it is usually legal to ban smoking, and in some states it is required by law in government offices).

It is not legal for an employer to ask you questions about your political or religious convictions. Further, it is also illegal to ask a woman if she is pregnant, if she intends to become pregnant in the near future, or anything related to child care (it is also illegal to ask men about their child care arrangements, but that rarely happens).

On Interviewing the Interviewer　There are two main purposes for an employment interview. One is for the employer to find out if you are right not only for the job but also for the organization. The other is for you to find out if the employer is right for you. The best way to do this is to make a list of characteristics important to you, as well as questions about the agency that come up when you respond to the interviewer (see earlier paragraph about preparing). Take the list with you to the interview and, toward the end, ask for any information you want that you have not already been given. Also, you can learn quite a bit about an agency by careful observation. Observe the physical surroundings and how members of the professional staff interact with each other and with support staff, such as secretaries and receptionists.

After the Interview We recommend following-up the interview with a brief note re-stating your interest in the position and thanking the interviewer for taking the time to consider you. Again, the letter should be typed. Since you will have met the person to whom the letter is addressed, it is crucial to have the correct name and title of that person on the letter. Follow-up letters should positive but not effusive: words such as "thrilled" and "ecstatic" are not appropriate. A sample letter is shown in Figure 3.

Follow-up phone calls are usually not a good idea, as you may be seen as overly eager. The exception to this rule is in the case where you have been told you will be contacted by a certain date and no contact has been made. In this case, it is reasonable to call and ask whether a decision has been made.

1234 Main Street
Anytown, USA 99999
September 25, 1988

Dorothy Sampson, Executive Director
Main Street Placement Agency
555 Central Avenue
Anytown, USA 99999

Dear Ms. Sampson;

I wanted to thank you again for the opportunity to meet with you and the placement staff this morning. I do feel I could make a positive contribution to your program, and look forward to hearing from you in the near future.

Sincerely,

Martin J. Duran

Figure 3. Follow-up letter.

Exercises

7-3. Make a list of the following:
    a. Important things you want to ask when you interview for a job
    b. Important things you want to look for in an organization when you go for an interview (e.g., the amount of supervision and feedback that is provided, the opportunity for advancement, the provision of professional training).

PLANNING FOR PROFESSIONAL DEVELOPMENT

Before you can plan for your professional development, you must be able to distinguish what you can do and do know from what you cannot do and do not know. Two categories of things you may need or want to learn include the skills you need to perform your present responsibilities and the skills you want to acquire so that you can expand professionally. Identifying skills you need to perform your current job can be unpleasant, because it involves admitting that you may have made mistakes, or that there are things you do not know. Many professionals in human services find it difficult to objectively review their own professional skills and identify their own deficiencies.

In the course of planning for your professional development, it is important to remember the difference between knowledge and skills. If you want to find out about new approaches to counseling, or the latest research on serving people with physical disabilities, you are interested in acquiring new knowledge. If you want to learn how to use a new therapeutic technique, you are interested in learning new skills. Classes and lectures are good ways to increase your knowledge. The only effective way to learn a new skill is to find someone who has the skill and who will provide you with lots of feedback about technique and what you are doing correctly and what you need to change. Often, the person who gives you feedback and suggests new directions for growth is called a "mentor." It is also helpful to observe someone effectively using the skill you want to learn, but this is not a substitute for getting feedback on your own performance.

It can be difficult, particularly in small agencies or in small communities, to find opportunities for professional development. Frequently, there is little money available to send you to formal training programs, particularly if these are not availiable locally. Below is a list of commonly used formal and informal ways to develop professionally.

Formal Approaches to Professional Development

Join a Professional Organization   Professional organizations offer several paths to development. Many of them publish journals or newsletters that can keep you abreast of current developments in your field. Most professional organizations hold annual conventions where you may hear speakers and meet other people who share your interests. The larger organizations usually have state and/or regional chapters that hold annual meetings closer to home and are therefore less expensive to attend than national meetings. Some professional groups also offer continuing education programs and send notices to all members. Another benefit of membership in a large national professional group is that other organizations and publishers often buy their mailing lists. Thus, if you belong to one group, you are likely to get notices of meetings and new materials from many different sources.

One useful resource for identifying professional organizations that may be of interest to you is A. T. Kruzas's *Social Service Organizations and Agencies Directory* (1982).

There are hundreds of professional human services organizations in the United States. A selection of these are listed in the appendix at the end of this chapter.

Go Back to School   There are a great variety of college and university programs aimed at the working professional. In many locations there are master's programs that offer classes primarily on evenings and weekends so that people who work full-time are able to attend. There are also programs that allow you to attend full-time for a few weeks every year and do the remainder of your work via correspondence. If you are interested in going back to school part-time, speak with other people in your field, and consult the resources of your professional organizations and of your public library to determine what is available. Also, find out if your employer offers any financial support for additional schooling.

Attend Workshops and Seminars   If you live in a metropolitan area, chances are you will find numerous opportunities to attend short workshops and seminars. These programs usually range from a half-day to several days in length, and can cost anywhere from $25 or $30 to $500 for a 4- or 5-day course. The quality of short workshops and seminars can vary widely. Before you invest your time and money, particularly if you will have to travel and pay for lodging, try to find other professionals who have attended courses sponsored by the same instructors. Ask them what topics were covered and what they got out of those courses (they may not have wanted what you do, so it is important to ask what was done as well as whether it met their needs). Many human services agencies do have budgets (not large) for staff development, and may be willing to pay part or all of the cost of a workshop or course.

Informal Approaches to Professional Development

Use Your Library   Almost every public and university library in the country has the ability to help you request a computer search on a topic of interest to you. Usually the library has a staff member who can advise you of the cost, and can help you list descriptor words for your topic and decide which databases to search. These searches typically cost between $10 and $40, and result in a list of references on the topic of interest. Then, if your local library does not have the references you want, it probably has an interlibrary loan department that will search nationally for your reference. If you have access to a college or university library, it will have a current journals room where you can browse through a variety of publications at no cost.

Use Your Colleagues   Almost everyone with whom you work has a skill that may be useful to you. Observe your colleagues and ask yourself what results they produce and what skills they have that you value. Then ask them for help in learning those skills. This can be a touchy request, because it means asking people to look at your deficits rather than your strengths. The best way we know to make feedback easier to hear and use is, as we discussed in Chapter 6, to make it proactive. That is, ask your colleagues to tell you what skills you need to use more often, not what is awful and what you should stop doing.

Find a Mentor   The dictionary defines a mentor as a trusted counselor, guide, tutor, or coach. A mentor is someone who can help you develop professionally. This person is therefore usually someone who has more skill, knowledge, or expertise than you do in at least one area of professional functioning. A mentor can teach you implicitly or explicitly. Implicit teaching is teaching by example: you watch the person and observe what he or she does. Explicit teaching is just that: the mentor instructs you and gives you feedback on how well you are doing.

You cannot require anyone to be your mentor, particularly of the explicit variety. However, you can carefully observe people you meet during your work, both within and from outside of your agency (don't forget your supervisor is a potential mentor), and look for those persons with skills or characteristics you wish to acquire. You may identify a prospective mentor by approaching an individual who has a specific skill you want to learn, or they may possess something more global, such as a style you want to emulate. Also, you are most likely to learn from a person if you see yourself as similar to her or him in some way.

Once you have found a possible mentor, ask for assistance. Most professionals, if they can spare the time, are happy to help less experienced colleagues broaden their skills. Mentors can be particularly useful by expanding your perspective on service delivery and by helping you to examine future options that differ from your present position. One caution about mentors: nearly all of us need more than one mentor during the course of our careers, and we often need more than one mentor at the same time. This is because no one person is likely to have all the answers or be able to provide a complete overview of all the possibilities open to you.

Start a Local Network Perhaps you work in a very small agency where there are only a handful of other staff members. There may be skills you want to learn that none of your co-workers will be able to teach you. In that case, start finding ways to learn from your colleagues at other agencies. There are a variety of ways to proceed, from having lunch periodically with one or more people from other organizations, to actually starting a local or state chapter of a professional organization.

Exercises

7-7. Find out, by talking to other people in your field, going to the library, or writing for information, about at least two professional organizations or university programs that might contribute to your professional development.
7-8. Do at least one of the following:
    a. Have your library run a computer search for you on a topic of professional interest.
    b. Identify a skill one of your colleagues (e.g., co-worker, supervisor, support staff member, or a person from another department) could teach you that you want to learn. Arrange to be taught that skill.
    c. Identify at least two people who work in other agencies in your community who have skills you want to learn. Meet with them to discuss your interest.

A FINAL NOTE ON PROFESSIONAL DEVELOPMENT

It is natural to prefer to concentrate on the parts of your job that are rewarding, including those activities that result in your professional growth. Do remember, as you plan for your professional development, that your employer's priorities for you may be different from your own. Most employers do support professional development, but they will expect employees to fulfill the basic responsibilities of their position before they focus on expanding their skills.

MORE TALES OF DIANA

Two months later: Diana and her discussion group meet again, as they have regularly for the past 3 months. Everyone has read *"Human services? . . . That must be so rewarding"* and all have worked through the exercises in Sections I, II, and III. Diana, smiling, tells the group: "I was so close to leaving human services before we started meeting. This book has helped me really look at who I am and why I am a probation officer."

"Best of all, having the support of this group has helped me take charge of my professional career. It's so reassuring to know that other people have the same problems and get the same rewards I do. I'm going to work through the next chapter on Stress Management, but I feel like this group is one of my best ways to manage stress! Would you be willing to keep meeting once a month to keep that support going"?

The group agrees to continue meeting and Bob offers his place for the next session, saying: "It's great being part of this motley crew— I've actually tried some of this stuff and it helps my attitude toward my job a whole lot."

PROFESSIONAL ORGANIZATIONS

American Association for Marriage and Family Therapy
924 W. Ninth
Upland, CA 91786

American Association of Children's Residential Centers
P.O. Box 14188
Washington, D.C. 20044

American Association on Mental Retardation
1719 Kalorama Road, N.W.
Washington, D.C. 20009

The American Correctional Association
4321 Hartwick Road, Suite L208
College Park, MD 20740

American Federation of Teachers
555 New Jersey Avenue, N.W.
Washington, D.C. 20001

American Mental Health Counselors Association
5999 Stevenson Avenue
Alexandria, VA 22304

American Physical Therapy Association
1111 N. Fairfax Street
Alexandria, VA 22314

Association for Behavior Analysis
Department of Psychology
Western Michigan University
Kalamazoo, MI 49008

The Association for Persons with Severe Handicaps
7010 Roosevelt Way, N.E.
Seattle, WA 98115

Association for the Advancement of Behavior Therapy
15 West 36 Street
New York, NY 10018

Council for Exceptional Children
1920 Association Drive
Reston, VA 22091

Gerontological Society of America
1411 K Street, N.W.
Washington, D.C. 20005

National Association for Rights, Protection, and Advocacy
M. Reneé Bostick
Ohio Legal Rights Service
8 East Long Street, 5th Floor
Columbus, OH 43266-0523

National Association of Social Workers
1425 H Street, N.W.
Washington, D.C. 20005

National Council on the Aging
600 Maryland Avenue, S.W.
Washington, D.C. 20024

National Education Association
1201 16th Street, N.W.
Washington, D.C. 20036

National Mental Health Association
1021 Prince Street
Alexandria, VA 22310

National Rehabilitation Association
633 S. Washington Street
Alexandria, VA 22314

Western Gerontological Society
833 Market Street, Suite 516
San Francisco, CA 94103

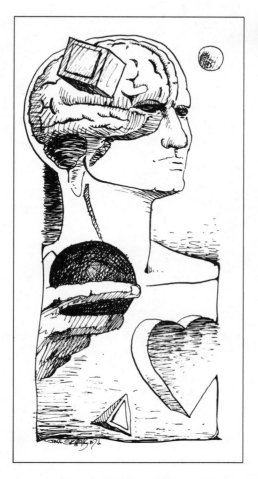

Again, HUMAN

CHAPTER 8

STRESS MANAGEMENT

OR

Mama Never
Told Me There'd Be Days Like This

OBJECTIVES

To be able to:
1. Identify some common negative reactions to stress.
2. Describe the characteristics of an effective approach to stress management.
3. Describe typical stress management tactics.
4. Develop a personal stress management plan.

If you are alive, there is stress in your life. According to Selye (1976), stress is "the nonspecific response of the body to any demand made on it." When people talk about being under a great deal of stress, or of being "stressed out," they mean they are feeling the negative effects of demands placed on them. In human services, professionals who are responding very negatively to stressors often say that they are "burned out." However, stress does not have to be consistently negative, nor does it have to have negative effects on you. This chapter is about negative reactions to stressors, what causes the reactions, and how to both minimize negative reactions and learn positive ones.

The authors' basic assumption is that people who work in the human services are "only human." This sounds so obvious it is almost silly to say it. However, consider some of the myths present in American society about human services workers. The myths suggest they are superhuman:

They are professionals who are above reproach
Their work provides them with inherent, infinite personal rewards
They are miracle workers
They remain calm at all times
They place the feelings of those they serve above their own
They love all those they serve
They have no favorites among those they serve
They know all of the answers
They cope with life without stress, anxiety, or conflict

(adapted from Greenberg, 1984)

These myths are not just silly, but sometimes dangerous. They become dangerous if we try to live up to them, refusing to acknowledge that we cannot be perfect. In fact, people with jobs that require that they have substantial responsibility for the welfare of others display an increased incidence of stress-related illnesses (Anderson, 1978). This chapter is about working in human services and being human (but not superhuman).

Effects of Stress

We have the same physiological responses to potential dangers that our ancestors had. As in prehistoric cultures, we experience increases in blood sugar and oxygen flow, in blood pressure, and in stomach acid. In extreme cases, adrenaline is released into our bloodstreams (Gardner & Chapman, 1985). These responses were very adaptive during an earlier evolutionary time: they prepared the person to react quickly to immediate physical danger in ways commonly referred to as either flight or fight. Today, we have the same physiological responses to other, less immediately dangerous stressors. For example, driving in rush-hour traffic can result in the same responses as being faced by a wild bull (e.g., increased heart beat, shortening of breath) (Kirsta, 1986).

These physiological reactions, if they occur often to someone who has not learned how to cope with them, can result in a variety of unpleasant effects. The way to prevent those effects is to learn skills to minimize or prevent stress. In general, you will need to be able to:

1. Find out whether you are exhibiting any of the typical negative effects of stress.
2. Identify possible causes of any negative stress symptoms you have.

3. Learn how to change yourself and/or your environment in ways that will reduce or eliminate your negative stress symptoms.

This chapter is about learning these three skills. The first section addresses ways to identify the negative effects stress can have on you.

The long-term negative effect of stress is physical illness. Some illnesses or physical problems that can be induced or aggravated by stress reactions are:

Acne	Fatigue
Alcoholism	Frigidity
Allergies	Headache
Asthma	Heart conditions
Colitis	Insomnia
Constipation	Obesity
Dermatitis and eczema	Peptic ulcers
Diabetes	Rheumatoid arthritis
Diarrhea	Sexual dysfunction

(adapted from Greenberg & Valletutti, 1980)

Fortunately, there are a host of physical, cognitive, and emotional warning signs that appear before one becomes seriously ill in response to stress. Different people display different warning signals: you may not have the same symptoms as the person in the next office, who has an ulcer, but you also may be at risk for physical illness. Typical physical warning signs of negative stress reactions are:

Alcohol dependency	Impulsive eating
Diarrhea, indigestion, vomiting	Muscle spasms
	Nausea
Drug addiction	Pain in back, neck, chest
Dry throat and mouth	Psychoses
Excessive weight change	Sexual dysfunction
	Shortness of breath
Excessive nervous energy	Sleeplessness
	Stuttering
Fatigue	Sweating
Fainting	Tooth grinding
Headaches	Trembling
High blood pressure	

(adapted from Greenberg & Valletutti, 1980)

Typical emotional, cognitive, or behavioral signs of negative stress reactions are:

Anxiety
Apprehension about
    approaching
    weekends and
    vacations
Constant uneasiness
Depression
Emotional outbursts
Feeling of rejection
Feeling of failure

Frustration
General boredom
Habitual or suppressed anger
General irritability
Impulsive behavior
Inability to concentrate
Inability to laugh
Irrational fears
Lack of control
Nightmares
Recurring sense of hopelessness

(adapted from Greenberg & Valletutti, 1980)

If you have any of these signs of a negative stress reaction for a prolonged period of time, consult your primary care physician. If your physician does not find a disease or other organic cause of your stress reactions, you may wish to consult a mental health professional for assistance in developing stress management skills. In addition, any behavior that indicates you are not acting like yourself may be an adverse reaction to stress. Further, consistently acting out of character is a serious warning sign of decreased ability to cope and should not be ignored (Kirsta, 1986).

BUT I FEEL FINE!

Right now you may not have any negative reactions to stress, either because there is not a great deal of tension in your life, or because you have developed good stress management skills. In either case, if you are feeling fine, you may wonder if there is any reason to bother reading this chapter. But it is when you are doing well that is the best time to: 1) review what you are doing well, and 2) identify any new stress management skills you may want to acquire. Becoming good at managing possible causes of stress in your life has been called "stressproofing" (Kirsta, 1986).

Stressproofing is particularly useful if you are at risk for illness due to stress in your life. The Holmes Rahe Scale (see Table 1) lists 41 positive and negative common life events that require adjustment and affect your risk of illness (Holmes & Rahe, 1967). A score of over 300

Table 1. The Holmes and Rahe Social Readjustment Rating Scale

Life event	Lifechange units
Death of spouse	100
Divorce	73
Marital separation	65
Imprisonment	63
Death of close family member	63
Personal injury or illness	53
Marriage	50
Dismissal from work	47
Marital reconciliation	45
Retirement	45
Change in health of family member	44
Pregnancy	40
Sexual difficulties	39
Gain of new family member	39
Business readjustment	39
Change in financial state	38
Change in number of arguments with spouse	35
Major mortgage	32
Foreclosure of mortgage or loan	30
Change in responsibilities at work	29
Son or daughter leaving home	29
Trouble with in-laws	29
Outstanding personal achievement	28
Spouse begins or stops work	26
Begin or end school	26
Change in living conditions	25
Revision of personal habits	24
Trouble with boss	23
Change in work hours or conditions	20
Change in residence	20
Change in schools	20
Change in recreation	19
Change in church activities	19
Change in social activities	18
Minor mortgage or loan	17
Change in sleeping habits	16
Change in number of family reunions	15
Change in eating habits	15
Vacation	13
Christmas	12
Minor violation of the law	11

Directions: Check each of the items on the list which have occurred in your life within the past 12 months. Then add the points associated with each of those items.

If you have over 300 points, you have a greatly increased risk of illness. 150–299 reduces the risk by 30%, and less than 150 involves a small chance of illness.

Note. From "The Social Readjustment Rating Scale" by T.H. Holmes and R.H. Rahe, 1967, *Journal of Psychosomatic Research, 11,* pp. 213–218. Copyright © 1967 by Pergamon Journals Limited. Reprinted by permission.

points in one year greatly increases your chance of illness. A score of 150–299 reduces the risk by 30%, and less than 150 involves a small chance of illness. However, even if you are at great risk due to major changes in your life, you can reduce that risk through the use of effective stress management tactics.

Developing a Stress Management Plan

> " To ignore the impact of stress . . .
> is a mild and slow form of suicide."
> (Greenberg & Valletutti, 1980, p.9)

The rest of this chapter is about managing stress in ways that reduce its negative effects. No one has exactly the same needs for stress management, so no two stress management plans will be alike. Thus, this chapter does not provide you with a list of things you should do to manage stress in your life. Instead, the following are provided: 1) a general strategy for developing a stress management plan that fits you, and 2) a discussion of tactics some people find useful for stress management.

Successful stress management will be more likely if you follow these guidelines:

1. *Start small.* We are all familiar with the person who makes a resolution to start the New Year off by making a major improvement in his or her life, but never carries it through. That is because real, permanent change does not occur in dramatic ways; instead, it occurs in a series of small steps that are manageable one at a time (Jaffe & Scott, 1984). For instance, a major career change might start with updating your resumé.
2. *Do something now.* Change in how you manage stress, like any other change, requires action; merely thinking about it is not enough (and it may increase the stress in your life). Your first attempt may not be successful, but you will have begun the habit of actively working to manage the stress in your life. Examples of beginning attempts at stress management are: taking 5 minutes for yourself when you first get home from work, walking for 10 minutes every day during your lunch break, and closing the door to your office for 5 minutes of daydreaming time.
3. *Set clear, specific goals* (Jaffe & Scott, 1984). For instance, you might decide your goal is to walk for 10 minutes during your lunch break at least three times a week, starting next Monday.
4. *Set proactive goals.* You may want to stop blaming yourself, stop

losing your temper, or stop trying to control everything, but you will not be successful unless you learn what to do instead (Bernstein et al., 1981). "Things to do" might include: 1) learning to analyze what happened when things go wrong and learning from your analysis instead of blaming yourself, 2) taking a deep breath and counting to ten so that you control your temper when you feel yourself starting to get angry, or 3) identifying at least one thing at work every day that you cannot control, and saying to yourself: "I can't do anything about that, and it's okay that I can't control it."

5. *Start from where you are, not from where you want to be.* Suppose your long-term goal is to engage in aerobic exercise a minimum of six times a week, for at least 45 minutes each time, but you are currently not exercising at all. Start by comparing your progress to where you have been, not where you want to go. A week in which you exercised 20 minutes for 3 days is not good if you compare it to your long-term goal, but it is terrific if you compare it to your starting point!

6. *Start working with what is most important to you.* If you start working with what is most important to you, you will be taking advantage of your strongest motivation for change.

7. *Make changes one at a time.* (Jaffe & Scott, 1984) Do not, for example, try to quit smoking, go on a diet, and quit drinking all at the same time.

8. *Plan ways to manage stress.* If part of your stress management plan is to spend more time with supportive friends with very busy schedules, make arrangements with them to go to dinner or a movie instead of waiting until the last minute and finding everyone busy.

9. *Make it easy to manage stress.* For instance, it may be easier to exercise in a health club by yourself than to try to schedule a handball court and partner. Or, it may be even easier to buy an exercise bike and work out at home.

10. *Look for ways to reward yourself for doing good work and for doing effective stress management.* Plan the reward you will give yourself when you complete an important project. Make signs, graphs, or public announcements each time you complete another step in a larger project. Remind yourself of all the things you are doing to take care of yourself.

11. *Pick stress management techniques likely to work for you.* If you hate outdoor exercise, select an aerobic activity such as swim-

ming in a pool, running on an indoor track, or cycling on an exercise bike. If large parties are events you wish to avoid, plan social evenings with small groups of friends.

12. *Look for ways to take control of your life, no matter how small.* Rearrange the furniture in your office, sit in a new place at a regular meeting, decide when you want to return a call. There *are* many ways you can control your life.

13. *Do it every day: new stress management skills require constant practice (Forman & Cecil, 1985).* The more often you have reacted to stress in a way that makes things worse, the more likely you are to react that way in the future. Thus, daily practice is necessary to learn the new skill well enough so that it will replace your old, dysfunctional reactions to stress. You may want to keep a card on your desk or in a pocket so that you can make a tally mark every time you practice your new stress management skill. This can help remind you to practice and can show you your progress.

14. *Finally, reassess your stress management skills and your need for them regularly.* Whenever there is any sort of major change in your life, sources of stress are likely to change. Some of the changes will be toward less stress, others toward more.

The rest of this chapter discusses causes and ways of managing stress as it relates to physical and mental well-being, environment, support systems, work, and personal growth.

PHYSICAL WELL-BEING

In general, the better you are at taking care of your body, the less stressed you will feel. The reason for this is simple: if you feel good physically, you will feel better able to respond to sources of stress in your life. If you do not feel good, your ability to respond effectively to stressful situations will be impaired. For instance, everyone has experienced the effects a headache or lack of sleep can have on productivity and tolerance.

Four Steps toward Improving Stress Management

There are four basic steps to follow to improve both overall health and the ability to manage stress.

Eat Well, and Eat At Least Three Meals a Day   There are four food elements that are particularly likely to interfere with your ability to manage stress: caffeine, sugar, salt, and alcohol. These are often called "mood foods" because they can have a significant effect on your mood and thus your ability to stay calm under stress (Kirsta, 1986). Caffeine has a speed effect, and too much of it can make you jumpy and irritable. Sugar leads to a quick high followed by a quick low. Too much salt will lead to excessive water retention and a bloated feeling. Alcohol can act temporarily as a stimulant, but will act as a powerful depressant with continued consumption (Kirsta, 1986).

Therefore, the less you use these four foods, and the more you eat a balanced diet, the better you will feel and the more able you will be to cope with daily stress (for more specifics on eating well, see Brody, 1985).

Exercise Regularly There are three components to physical fitness: flexibility, strength, and cardiovascular endurance. Two common ways to develop flexibility are through yoga or stretching calisthenics. Strength can result from activities such as weight lifting or calisthenics. Aerobic exercise such as aerobic dance, running, swimming, walking, or bicycle riding are needed for cardiovascular fitness. Consistent practice in one of the martial arts such as karate can improve all three fitness components. The most important aspect of any fitness plan is consistency: no exercise will be effective unless you do it regularly. One very useful way to encourage yourself to exercise regularly is to set a regular appointment with yourself to exercise and keep it as faithfully as you would mealtimes, bathing, or a date with a friend.

Have Regular Checkups Many physical illnesses can be treated and cured if they are identified early. Checkups will help determine whether a symptom you may be manifesting—such as extreme fatigue—is caused by working too hard, or by a physical disorder that can be treated medically.

Relax Regularly

> **"**Discipline does not disappear forever,
> but she does take vacations from time to time.**"**
>
> (Gendler, 1984, p. 11)

> **"**(Justice Louis) Brandeis was once criticized for taking a short vacation just before the start of an important trial. 'I need the rest,' explained Brandeis. 'I find that I can do a year's work in eleven months, but I can't do it in twelve.'**"**
>
> (Fadiman, 1985, p. 76)

Many people find it difficult to relax. They have so much to occupy their thoughts that they never stop trying to solve problems, regardless of whether the problems are professional or personal. Also, many people have not taken the time and learned the skills to physically relax. Failure to relax increases the stress one feels, both mentally and physically.

There are more ways to relax than the authors can possibly list here. Different strategies work for different people, and the amount and type of relaxation one needs varies from person to person. Vacationing is the most popular way to relax, particularly when it consists of sitting in a boat holding a fishing rod, or doing some other similarly slow-paced, unpressured activity. While longer vacations of 1–2 weeks are the norm, some people find several 4- or 5-day vacations throughout the year more relaxing than one long break. While vacations are often relaxing, sometimes they can be a source of stress. This is particularly likely if you try to take a vacation you cannot afford, or if people spending vacation time with you have different expectations from yours about what is going to happen. Vacations occur infrequently, so most of us also need ways to relax in our everyday lives.

It can be difficult to identify the outcomes of working with people, and equally difficult to figure out who is responsible for which outcomes. Human services workers sometimes are not able to point to a concrete outcome and say: "I did that." This is one of the reasons people whose work is largely verbal and not physical often relax by working with their hands. Gardening, woodworking, and cooking are popular examples.

When you are very busy with work, it is easy to forget to take time to relax, or even to forget how to relax. Formal approaches to relaxing and stepping back from daily pressures can be useful ways to interrupt this cycle. Some people meditate daily. Others use a technique called progressive muscle relaxation (Bernstein & Borkovec, 1973).

Progressive relaxation can be an important tool because it specifically teaches you to substitute a relaxation response for tension in your body. Relaxation training involves learning to tense and relax various muscle groups while learning to tell the difference between how tension feels and how relaxation feels. This may sound silly, but many of us do not have the ability to distinguish between tension and relaxation in our own bodies. Usually, the initial training of this technique is conducted by a skilled trainer, often a trained therapist. The person practices the tensing and relaxing sequence at home and/or at work, often with the aid of a cassette tape with recorded instructions.

Next, relaxing the sequence of muscles is practiced without tensing first. Finally, the person learns to associate the feeling of deep relaxation with a verbal cue such as the word "calm" (Forman & Cecil, 1985). Progressive relaxation can be a powerful aid to regular relaxing. It is not, however, a skill you can teach yourself. If you are interested, do find a trainer. Often, they are associated with health maintenance organizations or behavior therapy groups.

Exercises

8-1. Consider how well you take care of yourself physically.
   a. What do you do or not do about your physical health that usually leads to more stress for you?
   b. What are your best stress management skills with respect to your physical health?
   c. What stress management skills would you like to improve with respect to your physical health?

YOUR PHYSICAL ENVIRONMENT

The sight, sound, smell, and feel of your physical environment can increase or reduce stress levels. Following are some of the ways people try to make their physical environments more comfortable both at home and at work:

1. Sight. Hang pictures or other things you like to look at on the walls. Paint the walls or furniture a pleasing color. Put something you like to look at on your desk. Arrange things in your home or office in a way you find appealing. Make the lighting as pleasant and easy on your eyes as possible.
2. Sound. Play music you find relaxing or calming, shut your door to avoid unpleasant sounds, hang drapes to absorb sound. If you share a large open office that is noisy, wear ear plugs when you want to concentrate.
3. Smell. Fight pollution by keeping house plants, flowers, bowls of water, humidifiers, and/or air cleaners in your office.
4. Touch. Obtain comfortable furniture, particularly your office chair. Many people find chairs designed especially for back comfort important.

Exercises

8-2. Consider how well you take care of yourself with respect to your physical environment.

a. What do you do about your physical environment that usually leads to more stress for you?

b. What are your best stress management skills with respect to your physical environment?

c. What stress management skills would you like to improve with respect to your physical environment?

THOUGHTS AND STRESS

> "Worry has written the definitive work on nervous habits."
>
> (Gendler, 1984, p. 3)

> " Guilt is the prosecutor who knows how
> to make every victim feel like the criminal."
>
> (Gendler, 1984, p. 25)

Often stress is self-created. Remember, stress is our reaction to the demands placed on us. Sometimes we create negative stress for ourselves by not taking care of our bodies. Sometimes we create stress for ourselves by repeating thoughts that are irrational and counterproductive. Below you will find a list of common irrational thoughts. This list was compiled by Dr. Rian McMullin primarily from surveys and clinical observations by dozens of therapists, guidance counselors, special educators, psychiatric nurses, social workers, and other mental health specialists. McMullin also took items from Ellis and Harper's *A New Guide to Rational Living* (1976) and Hauck's *Rational Management of Children* (1967). These thoughts are not irrational under all circumstances, but people often have them under conditions that make them irrational.

Common Irrational Thoughts

1. People must always love me or I will be miserable.
2. Making mistakes is terrible.
3. It is terrible when things go wrong.
4. My emotions can't be controlled.
5. Self-discipline is too hard to achieve.
6. I must always depend on others.
7. My childhood will always dominate my behavior as an adult.
8. I believe there is a single perfect solution for my problem and all I have to do is find it.
9. I am an exceptional person (prince in disguise or a superwoman)

and require special privileges and favors. I shouldn't have to live within the limits and restrictions of ordinary mortals.

10. Beliefs held by respected authorities or society must be correct and therefore shouldn't be questioned.

11. If others criticize me I must have done something wrong.

12. I can't help what I think. If I think there is something wrong with me, then there is.

13. To be a good, moral, worthwhile person, I must help everyone who needs it. (Many mental health specialists said they believed this at the beginning of their careers.)

14. To be a manly man or a feminine woman, my sexual performance must always be outstanding, every time with every partner. Any inability to do so means I am a failure or a homosexual. (Ellis and other sex therapists report many clients have this thought.)

15. If I ever get anxious, fearful, or depressed, then I very likely will go crazy.

16. There is one true love and the person I am dating is it for me. If she or he ever leaves me, I might as well pack it in. (From counselors in college counseling centers.)

17. I ought to and must solve my problems quickly and without a great deal of effort.

18. It is the therapist's responsibility to solve my problems. She's the doctor, isn't she? You cure me and I'll sit here and watch. (Over 20 therapists sent this one.)

19. Strong, healthy, stable people solve their own problems. If you ask for help, you are weak, sick, or a coward.

20. If I don't want to do something, I can't do it. I just have to wait around until the mood hits me before I can take action. (From counselors helping students improve their study habits.)

21. If something is possible, it is probable.

22. The whole community is watching what I am doing. They are evaluating how well I do.

23. Before I make a decision, I must have a guarantee that it is the right one.

24. I should be like others.

25. A person shouldn't try to change their thoughts or feelings because they are natural and genuine to them.

26. In order to solve my problems, I must know the exact origin of them.

27. I should get very angry when people don't trust me, even when they don't know me.

28. I should feel happy and contented all the time.
29. I have a secret, hidden self inside of me that is sinister and could explode.
30. Working to solve my problems is more dangerous than doing nothing.
31. It's unfair that the world is not the way I would like it to be.
32. I am not responsible for what happens to me. Others are at fault when things go wrong for me.
33. I must control my anxiety constantly. Otherwise, it will overcome me and make me into a psychotic or cause me to do insane things.
34. I won't listen to therapists, because there is absolutely nothing they can tell me about myself that I don't already know.
35. I can't accept myself unless I have self-confidence.
36. I have never lived up to my potential.
37. I am unlucky.
38. When I trust someone, they always seem to let me down.
39. I should be different from what I am.
40. I am a born worrier.
41. If you really get to know me, you won't like me.
42. I can always tell what people think of me.
43. Happy people have free, uncontrolled emotions.
44. How bad I feel about losing someone shows how much I cared for them.
45. The stronger I feel something, the more likely it's true.

(Note. Adapted from *Talk sense to yourself: A guide to cognitive restructuring therapies* by R.C. McMullin, 1987. Reprinted by permission.)

We create stress for ourselves when we rehearse and endorse irrational and counterproductive thoughts. It sounds silly, but the way to stop yourself from perpetuating this type of useless pattern is to learn to think differently about difficulties. Three strategies you can use to help you cope with irrational thoughts are: counters, limiting when and where you worry, and thought-stopping.

Counters Counters are alternatives to your irrational thoughts that you create. For example, an irrational thought would be: "I have to serve everyone who needs help if I am to be a good and worthwhile helper." A counter to this would be: "I'm only one person, and it's okay if I do a good job of helping a few people. It's silly to think I can be a superperson and help everyone."

Here is a second example of a counter. Suppose your supervisor calls you into her office and tells you that while your work with people is very good, your reports are not as clearly written as they should be. She then gives you several examples of how to improve and offers to review and comment on draft versions of your reports. Here is one of the typical ways to make this situation worse by thinking irrational thoughts:

Boy, I've really screwed it up this time.
She must think I'm pretty stupid.
I'll never get a good letter of recommendation now.
I'm just doing a terrible job.
Nothing I can do pleases her.

Suppose you find yourself repeating the sequence of thoughts described above, and are feeling worse with each repetition. Consider the first thought in the example above: "I've really screwed it up this time." This thought may be true, but it is unlikely to make you feel better. A good question to ask yourself is: "What do I need to do to make myself feel better"? (If this thought helps you feel the way you want to feel, then you like feeling miserable, which is another problem.) You may decide that what will make you feel better is figuring out how to improve and thus avoid negative feedback in the future. What might you want to tell yourself instead? Here is one set of possible counters:

Boy, I really screwed that up.
But she did tell me what I do well.
I guess I need to do something about my report writing.
Well, she showed me how to improve.
I will set aside a little time every day to practice my reports.
Today I have 30 minutes free time from 2:00 till 2:30, so I'll practice
    then.
It's good to have a supervisor who will help me improve.

If you have a small number of irrational thoughts that bother you frequently, you may find it useful to write down your counters and keep them in a place where you can refer to them often (Ellis & Harper, 1976).

Limit When and Where You Worry   Most of us worry some of the time, and sometimes with good reason. However, worrying too often and in the wrong places can give us even more to fret about if we worry instead of working. Since it is unrealistic to plan to stop worrying altogether, an alternative strategy is to limit yourself to worrying only at certain times and in a limited number of places. For instance, you might decide to allow yourself to worry about what your supervisor thinks of you only during your morning coffee break. Even better, you might also decide that during the times you are allowed to worry, you must also think about how to improve so you will not have as much to worry about. Finally, an important part of this strategy is that you do not allow yourself to worry about your supervisor's opinion of you at any other time.

Thought-Stopping This is just what it says. You tell yourself loudly and definitely to "Stop"! thinking an irrational thought. It is particularly useful at times when you should be concentrating on something else and do not have time to work on counters. An important meeting is an example of a time you might want to use thought-stopping.

Exercises

8-3. Consider how well you take care of yourself with respect to your thoughts.
    a. What do you do about your thoughts that usually leads to more stress for you?
    b. What are your best stress management skills with respect to your thoughts?
    c. What stress management skills would you like to improve with respect to your thoughts?
8-4. Pick two irrational thoughts from the list above that you have regularly. For each one, write out at least two counters.

STRESS AT WORK

When stress at work affects you negatively, it can be the result of poor stress management on your part or poor management on the part of the organization. Here are some of the most important things the organization should be doing for you:

1. It should be clear to you what is expected of you (Greenberg & Valletutti, 1980).
2. It should be clear to you what authority you have and what authority you do not have. Your responsibilities should match your authority (Greenberg & Valletutti, 1980).
3. You should have some role in planning your contribution to the organization. This does not mean complete control, but it does

mean that you are included to some extent in the decision-making process (Greenberg & Valletutti, 1980).

4. You should be getting clear, regular feedback about what you have done well and what you need to do to improve.

Here are some of the things you should be doing at work to manage stress:

1. If you are not clear about what is expected of you, ask.
2. Associate primarily with people who are willing to try to solve problems, not with people who complain loudly but do not try to solve anything (Greenberg & Valletutti, 1980).
3. If you want more feedback, ask for it.
4. Do not try to do everything by yourself—if you need help, ask for it.
5. Learn your limits and do not take on more than you can competently handle.
6. Have fun at your job. Just because you do serious work does not mean you have to be serious all the time.

Exercises

8-5. Consider how well you take care of yourself at work.
   a. What do you do at work that usually leads to stress for you?
   b. Identify your best stress management skills with respect to your work.
   c. What stress management skills would you like to improve at work?

SUPPORT SYSTEMS

Most people choose to live and work with other people rather than in isolation. They desire the company and support of others. This section is about support: what it is and where one usually finds it.

Often, when "support" is mentioned, it is interpreted as "emotional support." In fact, there are many forms of support, including at least the following: 1) listening, 2) appreciation for our skills, 3) challenges to improve our skills, 4) emotional support, 5) reality testing (Gardner & Chapman, 1985), 6) challenges to work harder (Jaffe & Scott, 1984), and 7) technical assistance.

Each of us has a unique set of individual needs for support, in terms of what type of support we need, what people can provide it, and how many of them we look to for support. Also, each of us has different skills at providing various types of support for others. If you are going to manage the stress in your life successfully, you will need to know what types of support you need and who you want them from.

Support comes from a variety of sources. Most of us have different organizations and people to whom we turn for different forms of support. The most common sources are: 1) intimate relationships (spouses, partners), 2) family members, 3) friends, 4) colleagues, 5) professional organizations, 6) community organizations, and 7) support groups (adapted from Jaffe & Scott, 1984).

In general, getting and giving effective support requires that you know: 1) what kind of support you need, 2) from whom you can get support, 3) what kind of support you can give, and 4) to whom you can give support. Some ways to improve your support systems are:

Identify the people whose support is most important to you and tell them how much you appreciate their support

Plan your time so that as much of it as possible is spent with people who are supportive

Ask for the support you need

Give support to others

Decrease time spent with people who are not supportive (adapted from Jaffe & Scott, 1984).

Exercises

8-6. What kinds of support do you need? Rank the seven types of support described above in order of importance to you.

8-7. List at least one person from whom you get each type of support.

8-8. List three activities you enjoy that will improve your support systems (such as meeting new people or spending more time with people you care for); implement these activities.

PERSONAL GROWTH

People who work in human services spend much of their time meeting the needs of others. Sometimes we feel guilty about taking the time and energy to take care of ourselves. This is unfortunate, for in the long run we are not going to do the best job or be the best friends or partners we can be if we neglect ourselves. Following are additional methods people use to take care of themselves:

1. Get involved in a creative experience. Take up a craft, sing in a chorus, write poetry.

2. Spend time with people who do not work in human services. If you spend all your nonwork time with people who do human services work, you may forget that there are other ways of looking at the world. Exposure to a variety of people and ideas can be an exciting way of relaxing and refreshing yourself.
3. Spend some time alone. While individual tolerance levels differ, few of us want to spend every minute of our waking hours with other people.
4. Do something for someone else that has no connection with your work. Many people find personal fulfillment in volunteer work; human services professionals often do. Some of us do volunteer work related to human services, such as serving as a board member or helping with special recreational activities. Others prefer to volunteer in other ways, by doing things like working on political campaigns, volunteering in animal shelters, or supporting the arts.
5. Laugh a lot. The human condition can be painful and funny at the same time.

> "You get anything that true and
> you don't think it's funny, it'll kill you."
>
> (Rosalie Sorrels, 1985)

Exercises

8-9. Make a list of the things you do for your personal growth, and a second list of the things you would like to do for your personal growth but do not currently do.
8-10. Pick two changes you want to make in your life that will result in improved stress management. Make a plan for how you are going to make each change. Start implementing one of them.

STRESS AS A POSITIVE FORCE

As we noted earlier, stress can be a positive experience. Many of our responses to the demands placed on us are positive and are healthy for us physically and/or mentally. Often new challenges make us feel excited and glad to be alive. While this chapter has emphasized coping with negative stress reactions, please remember that some stress is healthy: only when you cannot cope effectively with the demands placed on you does it become negative.

CHAPTER 9

THE PROACTIVE HUMAN SERVICES PROFESSIONAL

OR

Putting It All Together

OBJECTIVE:

To be able to:

1.   Identify your long-term professional development goals.

This book, in summary, concerns the search for answers to the following questions:

What do I expect to get out of doing human services work?
What do I expect to accomplish?
What are, or should be, my values as I provide services?
How do I act while I provide services?
How do I manage the stress of working in human services?

Each of the chapters addresses one or more of these questions. This closing chapter is intended to bring those pieces back together in order to leave you with a holistic picture of human services as a career.

Human Services as a Career

Some people enter human services work intending to make it a career; others never planned such a long-term commitment, but it just seemed to happen to them. If a large part of your life is to be spent working in one of the human services, it is important to think of and approach your work as part of a career and a profession. This does *not* necessarily mean you must always be looking for the next career move or promotion, although you may wish to do so. Rather, it might be that you take your work seriously enough to plan for your own professional development. There is a myth that human services workers do not, and perhaps should not, think of themselves and their careers because they should be selfless people dedicating their lives to others. This is, in our opinion, a dangerous myth. If you do not take yourself seriously, you cannot be expected to take the people you serve seriously, and you cannot expect to be taken seriously as a human services professional.

One of the primary goals of this chapter is to convey what it takes to create a positive, fulfilling career in human services work. That is, we want to pull back from the specifics of the first eight chapters and take a broader look at human services careers, particularly as they progress over time. The authors enlisted three human services professionals to help us with that task by agreeing to be interviewed. Additionally, one of the authors was interviewed. Each was asked a series of questions concerning the ways in which their careers, goals, and expectations have developed and changed over time.

PROFILE: JUDITH HALASZYN

Judith Halaszyn, one of the authors of this book, is currently Assistant Residential Director for the Jefferson County Community Center for Developmental Disabilities.

What Degrees, Course Work, and Other Training Have You Had?

Most of my training has been on the job. I have been in human services since 1962, and until 1981, all my experience was in direct care. During those years, I attended numerous inservice training sessions and various in-house training programs that addressed everything from arts and crafts to behavior management techniques. Also, in the mid-sixties, I attended New Mexico State University part-time for several years and accumulated approximately 90 hours in secondary education, history, and science. In 1983, I finally received the push I needed to return to school and finish my bachelor's degree. I participated in the University Without Walls program at Loretto Heights College here in Denver. Through an innovative concept designed for the older, working person, I was able to design my areas of concentration and to study with two professionals in the community. By then, I had decided that my future was definitely in management and supervision. In 1984, I graduated with a B.A. with a concentration in organizational behavior management.

What Jobs Have You Held in Human Services?

I have been a direct care worker with a variety of populations. For 8 years, I worked in a treatment facility for court committed juvenile delinquents. Then, I worked in residential programs for emotionally disturbed children. From 1974 to 1978, I worked in a private institution teaching arts and crafts to developmentally disabled adults. I eventually developed this into an in-house cottage industry. This was the beginning of my association with developmental disabilities—an association which has continued to this day. It was the first of four direct services jobs I held that involved working with developmentally disabled people.

Then, for 3 years, I was responsible for the supervision and training of 20 full-time direct-care staff members for a large community-based residential program. It was the beginning of my interest in management. At first, I thought I would miss the daily client contact, and I still do. However, I took to the new position like a duck to water. People, whether staff or clients, are exciting and challenging, pushing me to be my best. Two years ago, I was promoted to assistant residential director. With that position has come a much greater involvement in personnel issues and in motivation of staff. Additionally, I am committed to developing excellence in the staff members for whom I am responsible. No two days are ever the same.

What Are Your Likes and Dislikes about Working in Human Services? How Have These Changed over the Years, if at All?

What I have always liked, and what has been my personal motivation to remain in the human services field, is the people. Plain and simple: I would go crazy if I spent my day with machines. I have been genuinely excited and pleased with the insight or progress achieved by someone with whom I have labored and struggled, and I have just as often been frustrated and impatient when those changes did not occur. Over the years, I have worked with some exceptional co-workers who have also been motivators and sources of support—people I have learned from.

In the past several years, what has changed is that I have more limited client contact, and I miss that. I have often found management of staff to be 1,000 times more frustrating than dealing with clients. However, it still gives me chills when I look at the overall excellence of the staff I have trained, knowing how far they have come. I realize my influence will ultimately have an impact on a greater number of clients through the staff that I have trained. I also still shudder over some of my poor judgments in hiring.

What Do You Want to Accomplish through Your Work? What Rewards Do You Wish to Receive? What Has Changed, if Anything?

What I want to accomplish has taken on a broader emphasis. It's no longer an individual as much as the system that I want to change. I have learned that it's when systems change that the greatest good for clients can be achieved. As an assistant administrator, I feel that my range of influence is greater, and that I am in a better position to advocate for staff as well as for programmatic needs. I want to share with new managers in other agencies the personnel expertise that I have developed so that they also can begin to create an environment of excellence. Too often, agencies forget about direct-care providers when they talk about professionalism and excellence. My approach is more grass roots: the professional expectations and the training toward excellence have to begin with the staff who actually work with our clients. However, philosophically, that commitment has to begin at the top of an agency.

Have You Found it Difficult to Balance Your Personal and Professional Lives? If So, What Works for You?

During the many years I worked in direct care, I did not feel the intrusion of work on my personal time. I was able to leave it behind. However, when I became a supervisor and was on-call after hours, it was a struggle. I found that I would work a 10- or 12-hour day and not use flex time, so I had to learn to set limits. It has been a gradual shaping process of: 1) telling myself that if it's not a life and death issue, it *can* wait, 2) having my home calls screened when I'm not on call, 3) not bringing paperwork home, and finally, 4) not talking about work in my time off. One extremely helpful factor for me is that, for the most part, the people I socialize with are not in human services. I find the juggling act is continuous, not one that you achieve, and it's set forever. The more I am able to mentally separate work time and personal time at the end of the day or week, the more refreshed and revitalized I am when I do return to work.

Is There Anything Else You Want to Convey to People Who Are Just Starting Out or Who Are Already in Human Services?

It's never easy, it's always changing, and you can never stop learning. This last point is especially important: don't let yourself stop learning and growing. Lastly, you will *never* be rich—but it's worth it!

Exercises

9-1. Consider these questions:
    a. Can you identify with any aspect of this interview?
    b. What lessons do you find in this interview that you think are important for human services professionals?

You may want to discuss each of these interviews with colleagues or classmates. We have found that individual reactions to each interview vary considerably. Thus, you may find a friend who gets very different messages from the interviews than you do.

PROFILE: DOUG BRADLEY

Doug Bradley is a special education teacher in a residential treatment program for children with emotional problems.

What Degrees, Course Work, and Other Training Have You Had?

My bachelor's degree is in psychology, and part of that was a two-year program in mental health work. My degree is from the University of Illinois at Urbana/Champaign. My master's degree is in educational psychology, and I also have an elementary school teaching certificate, both from the University of Colorado at Boulder. Right now, I'm working on an endorsement in teaching the educationally handicapped at the University of Colorado at Denver. Actually, I've taken enough courses that I can take the comprehensive exams this summer and get another master's in special education. I've already put in the time and money and what it boiled down to was writing comps, so I'll get that second master's. I'm also still a doctoral student in Educational Psychology at the University of Colorado in Boulder.

What Jobs Have You Held in Human Services?

After I got my bachelor's degree, I immediately came out to Denver and started working as a mental health worker at Children's Hospital. I was there for about 7 years. Now, I'm a teacher in a residential treatment center for emotionally disturbed children. I was pretty clear about the population I wanted to work with right away and for me that's just kids. I think you are stretching yourself to divide your work among child, adolescent, and adult psychology, and so children are first for me, and that was my choice even before the job at Children's. Children's Hospital was an ideal placement for me. We saw every diagnostic category that exists. Children are still my commitment, although some options for getting into adolescent work are opening up.

What Are Your Likes and Dislikes about Working in Human Services? How Have These Changed over the Years, if at All?

The most positive thing about the job is working with the kids. It always has been. When I was at Children's, as well as where I am working now, with a pretty severely disturbed population (maybe the most severe), there've been plenty of success stories. You see lots of progress with kids, and those definitely outnumber the ones that don't make any progress. In terms of what I'm shooting for in general: it's always been working with groups of kids. I never really bought the idea of individual hour-a-week therapy with these guys. In some isolated cases, it makes lots of sense. For the most part though, I'm not sure it does much but clear the diagnostic picture for the person that's spending the time with them.

My dislikes have always been the salary and the schedule. I guess that one of the reasons I wanted to get out of Children's was that we rotated all the shifts. Despite the salary of about 10 dollars an hour, working all shifts including nights, and sometimes having to cover twenty-four hours, got to be too much. Of course, I'm still in residential work, but I'm working straight days now as a teacher. That was definitely some of the motivation to get out of Children's.

Children's Hospital was the ideal place to get background, but there was no place else to go in that system. As a matter of fact, as an undergraduate I looked into getting my RN degree, but there was just too much extra work required to do it at the time. Part of going back to school was to think about the school psychology degree, and the more I got into that, the more I decided it was not a good decision for me. In school psychology programs, you're still doing bus duty, you're still meeting the kids individually, and you're writing up tests, so the amount of contact you have with the kids is not impressive. The whole idea of teaching special ed. made lots of sense to me because of the groups of kids. My present salary was actually a bit of a cut from what I was earning at Children's, but I guess I can't complain about the 3 months off in summer. Hopefully, I can improve the salary, but I don't see that changing too much very quickly.

The other thing I like is that I am working with a bunch of people my own age, and I don't think that's true of most jobs. Also, I've always had a good group of people to work with. I do think the field attracts some strange people who have come and gone over time, but most of my good friends and lasting relationships have been colleagues, so that's positive.

The only thing I can think of that's changed is that now it is less stressful. It was pretty stressful starting at Children's. Somehow, changing over to teaching, I noticed the same kind of ulcer symptoms for a little while. But something has changed—after the first year at both jobs I wasn't taking it home and things got a lot easier. I guess just knowing what to do, being comfortable on the job, and seeing kids always fitting the same mold, even though they're all different, helps. There are certain dynamics they all share, so that makes it much easier.

What Do You Want to Accomplish through Your Work? What Has Changed, if Anything?

I guess the decision about what I wanted to accomplish ever since way back was that I wanted to be working with kids and working with groups of kids. I made that decision knowing that was where the therapy was taking place and where change was happening. Most of the kids would be pretty fine in a one-to-one situation, and I had that in mind the whole time at Children's, because there wasn't a way to work with groups. I considered school psychology positions, but I realized they were dead ends, and wouldn't do anything for me teaching didn't. Part of that was I saw the salary schedule, the raises, and all the rest.

My attitudes haven't changed about doing psychotherapy or even individual therapy with some of the kids. I still think all the therapy that happens with them is in the group setting and in the classroom.

I've always had in mind to be working with a group of kids and designing the program of treatment at a residential treatment facility. I say residential because you have a better handle on the kids, but it could be a day treatment type thing too. That hasn't changed, though I'm not exactly sure where that's going to come into the picture and I don't see it happening real soon. I was qualified to teach before I got the teaching certificate, and qualified before I had done the other 3 years of schooling just for this extra endorsement. I think the same is true with the residential treatment thing: I'll have the qualifying experience before I actually have the credentials to be hired.

What Are the Rewards You Get from Your Work? How Have These Changed over the Years, if at All?

Well, when I started, the work and the paycheck were part of the reward. Feeling good about work just changes and comes and goes for a while. I was in a pretty special situation at Children's: we worked together so tightly and worked things out so well. It was ideal. There were periods of time when there were employees we had to get rid of, because their work was unsatisfactory, but most of the positives about work came from the co-workers. That hasn't changed. It's been the same the whole time and I think that's mostly where the reward comes from. Then there are all the rewards from the kids, not only seeing their growth, but also how much they get attached to you.

Have You Found it Difficult to Balance Your Personal and Professional Lives? If So, What Works for You?

It was difficult for about the first year—part of the trick was learning to literally leave it there and not think about it afterward. I like to think I've gotten good at that without creating so much distance that I'm not helping the kids. You have to have the relationship with them, because the alliance is part of what's going on. I noticed again when I started this other job that it can be very stressful. I guess part of it comes from stepping in front of ten kids with ten different dynamics going on. Now that I've adjusted to it, it hasn't been a problem. Of course, it's something that requires a conscious effort.

I'd really be in trouble without the support systems of some of the other adults that I work with; with these co-workers, I'm able to get off to the side, and in layman's language, talk about how crazy a kid's behavior has been and what a nut he is. Also, what I do now is all kinds of outside activities. I play softball, teach skiing, and play hockey. Teaching skiing is an interesting activity. The kids I teach are physically handicapped and that's the whole point. Otherwise, they are absolutely normal, so I enjoy that positive interaction with those kids a lot.

Is There Anything Else You Want to Convey to People Who Are Just Starting Out or Who Are Already in Human Services?

I think there are a lot of lousy jobs out there to avoid. I was out of a very sophisticated program at the University of Illinois stressing the professionalism of the mental health worker. But there are a lot of jobs for which "life experience," rather than specialized training, are sufficient. I think choosing the job is really critical—because there are so many dead-end ones. Make sure it's enough money and the kind of hours that you can live with first. Also, look at the people you're working with, not just the population of kids. As a matter of fact, I think the population of kids would be somewhat secondary.

For the person just starting out in the field, I'd let them know their schooling is not over with and to keep that in mind and to keep learning. I've been a perpetual student. I've been advised in the past to think about a facility that has lots of options for learning. Children's had lots of departments and expertise to tap into. I guess my advice to people would be to take advantage of connections and look into a sophisticated system with lots of resources, and keep up those support systems with other professionals.

Exercises

9-2. Consider these questions:
   a. Can you identify with any aspect of this interview?
   b. What lessons do you find in this interview that you think are important for human services professionals?

PROFILE: CHERYL LAMMERS

Cheryl Lammers is a probation officer in Jefferson County, Colorado.

What Degrees, Course Work, and Other Training Have You Had?

I have a B.A. in psychology and a minor in music (of all things!). I was originally a music major, then a biology major, and finally a psychology major. I began psychology with an interest in research and experimental psych., and ended with a desire to work with children. I explored music therapy and working with developmentally disabled people before landing in probation.

My course work emphasized developmental and clinical psych., with a special summer course in juvenile delinquency and forensic psychology. There was no criminal justice major available at the University of Denver, where I studied.

Since graduation from college, I have attended numerous seminars and inservice training sessions on topics such as: substance abuse, sexual offender dynamics and treatment, reality therapy, transactional analysis, professional liability, the theories of Stanton Samenow, forensic diagnostics, children's code (law) update, mid-life crisis, and the relationship between criminal behavior, bulemia, and anorexia.

Because probation deals with such a wide variety of people who have such diverse problems, it is important to know as much about as many areas of dysfunction as possible. Keeping current regarding community resources and trends in treatment is a major factor in successful human services work.

I also had some basic business courses, such as typing and accounting. Believe it or not, they have come in very handy! Human services agencies never seem to have adequate clerical help, and I have had to type my own reports more than once.

What Jobs Have You Held in Human Services?

I started right out of college in juvenile probation. I did internships while still in college, and I feel these are very valuable in helping a new graduate make a career choice. At the very least, internships let you decide what areas you definitely do not want to pursue. After 4 years as a juvenile probation officer, I moved to supervising adult offenders and took over coordination of the probation volunteer program. I have become much more active and knowledgeable in volunteer management in the last 2 years. Most areas of human services are more than willing to allow employees to develop creative programs (volunteer programs are one example), as long as the employee is attending to his or her assigned duties.

What are Your Likes and Dislikes about Working in Human Services? How Have These Changed over the Years, if at All?

I came to the human services field as a probation officer, armed with theories, college-formed opinions, and principles and ideas of how the judicial system was going to function. I enjoyed working with "difficult" cases, and spent many hours coordinating treatment plans and services for juvenile legal offenders. I was convinced that I wanted to work with juveniles until I died.

In college, there was a definite division between the behaviorists, the researchers, and the Freudians. I had chosen to identify with the Freudians. I believed very strongly in the Freudian principles and viewpoint, and I dealt with clients accordingly.

Looking back 8½ years: when I was a new probation officer, I saw human services as pretty clear-cut, black and white. In those days, the solutions were clearer, the sources and causes of the problems were clearer, and the course of action to be pursued was clearest of all. Unfortunately, "the system" wouldn't always cooperate, nor would the clients! A dose of reality was so disheartening to this naive college graduate!

I no longer enjoy spending hours with a noncooperative client. I still enjoy working on difficult cases, but I no longer "waste" time on lengthy treatment plans with unwilling, resistive clients who deny any problems or responsibility for any problems. There are certain options available in each situation. These options tend to overlap and/or have gaps in them. There is not always an applicable program available for a specific problem. Once the options are known, the client has certain choices.

It was startling to realize that not all people shared my value system! For example: while I may feel it is wrong for him or her to do so, a client may feel he or she has the right to continue breaking the law, drinking alcohol to excess, or using heroin. My job is to try to ensure that others are not hurt by a client's choice and that the client experiences the full impact of the consequences related to his or her choice. *I have learned not to care more about the outcome of a situation than the client cares.* Needless to say, at this point, some behaviorist philosophy was creeping into my chosen Freudian approaches.

Effective human services workers are knowledgeable in many areas. They are able to assess and define problems and are then able to choose, from the vast reservoir of theories, treatment modalities, and service agencies, the treatment that best meets the client's needs. This sounds so simple, but it is not. Theories change, as do agencies and available services. Appropriate referrals necessitate ongoing monitoring and training.

An unfortunate reality of human services work is that most human services agencies receive government funding at some level. Working in a bureaucracy where program funding, salaries—and even some agency policies—are determined by legislative allocations is often frustrating. Individual employee incentives are few, and salaries are most often determined by a set classification system rather than by amount or quality of work. I have watched co-workers and friends in other human services agencies leave their jobs, and even the human services field, due to their frustrations with the effects of bureaucratic politics on their agency policies and funding, and on their ability to work effectively with clients.

Human services jobs do not always fit the teachings of our youth: that if you work hard and do a good, conscientious job, good things will come to you. On the contrary, it is often the case that the harder you work, the higher the expectations of you become, but you will be paid the same as the guy next to you who does only what is required at a bare minimum!

What Do You Want to Accomplish through Your Work? What Rewards Do You Wish to Receive? What Has Changed, if Anything?

No longer do I wish to change the world. My goals have become more realistic and focused in relation to the confines and realities of the system in which I work. My rewards and satisfaction come from smaller scale accomplishments, such as getting one client plugged into a complete program of services that enables him to feel happier and more comfortable with the world around him. Similarly, I feel satisfaction when a client feels more in control of his or her life and future path.

I plan more carefully for goals to be reached in the years to come, and have learned to slow my pace in accordance with the snail-like pace of the governmental offices and agencies under whose guidelines I must operate. When I now look back $8^{1}/_{2}$ years, I can see my first 4 years as an orientation to the system in which I now operate. The next $4^{1}/_{2}$ years show a steady, but slow, improvement in services and lines of communication. This is due in part to my work and level of understanding regarding the realities of "the system."

I want to prevent people from becoming heavily involved in crime by showing them effective alternatives to their present and/or past coping techniques. I want to feel that I am at least partly responsible for keeping the system accountable (i.e., the criminal justice system and related agencies). If nothing else, I want clients to see and experience the consequences of their actions so that they may make informed choices. In some cases, I want the clients to know that there is someone who cares and will be honest and consistent in dealings with them.

I also work with community volunteers within the judicial system. I hope to see an accountable network of volunteer services recognized by the judicial system before I retire (or die). Working with judicial volunteers has been very rewarding. These people have become a support system for me, as they help to accomplish small goals to improve services within the judicial system. As our volunteer program has slowly expanded, it has become a political force that provides a powerful voice to elected officials.

Once a human services worker can identify "similar souls" in the community (and they are always there), these people can be organized into a very valuable support system and a very effective force for advocating needed changes. This type of support must be organized slowly and with foresight, to prevent formation of a radical and detrimental group.

In human services, workers sometimes feel isolated and alone. We forget that there are others (though not necessarily in a specific human services field) who share our views and ideals. These people may not have actual hours to contribute to improving the system, but they may be able to donate money or the political drive necessary to bring about desirable changes.

It has also become critical to me to see a more holistic view. In human services work, one can tend to focus only on one's clientele and their problems. One forgets the larger picture and may lose contact with the healthier part of society. This can give one a rather morbid and depressed view of the world. It is important to balance human service work with other interests that bring one healthier contacts with other individuals whose problems are not your primary concern.

For instance, it was so enlightening for me to speak at a local high school about the juvenile justice system. I saw kids who were actually planning to attend college! After 4 years of working with juvenile delinquents, my view had become skewed. I thought no young people were finishing high school, let alone considering college! This was a prime example of my human services work getting out of proportion and becoming too much of a priority!

Have You Found it Difficult to Balance Your Personal and Professional Lives? If So, What Works for You?

As a new probation officer, I used to spend many extra hours on client problems. I now believe clients must be given the opportunity to solve their own problems, and not having immediate access to me at all hours helps them to improve their own coping abilities. I am now able to tell a client who reaches me at night to call me in the morning, at work. Most problems can be dealt with the following day without a drastic change in the outcome. It also forces clients to plan ahead, because they know you are only available to them at certain specific times.

I have come to realize that many of my clients expect me to be available to them at all times. However, they do not reciprocate the courtesy. If a client wants my services, it will need to be under my terms, which are *very* reasonable! There are always those clients for whom I will go the extra mile, but there are *many* who, if given an inch, will take a mile!

Balancing my personal and professional life has been difficult, especially since the birth of my first child in 1986. My son really forced me to reevaluate and change my priorities. As I mentioned previously, having a healthy balance in one's life, just like a balanced diet, is essential to one's emotional and physical well-being, as well as being essential to survival in a human services field.

Specifically, I no longer work extra hours. I pay close attention to quitting time, and try to leave my work problems at the office. There is always tomorrow. I am fortunate to have a husband who was willing to give up his paid work to stay home with our son. So, the worry of day care has not been a problem for me. After working hours is my time for myself and my family. I try to give my family and myself the same quality of attention that I give to my clients during working hours.

Is There Anything Else You Want to Convey to People Who Are Just Starting Out or Who Are Already in Human Services?

I always advise new professionals to look carefully at the salary schedule for raises, and decide whether to stay before they get too well paid and can't afford to leave. What you need to do is pick a stopping point right before a scheduled big raise, and ask yourself: "Is this the organization, people, and work I want"?

Also, remember people will not always reward you for doing a good job, so you need to have your own ideals and principles to sustain you.

Exercises

9-3. Once more, consider these questions:
   a. Can you identify with any aspect of this interview?
   b. What lessons do you find in this interview that you think are important for human services professionals?

PROFILE: MARY ANNE HARVEY

Mary Anne Harvey is currently Executive Director of The Legal Center, a protection and advocacy organization for persons with disabilities.

What Degrees and What Other Training Do You Have? What Jobs Have You Held in Human Services?

I have a bachelor's degree in English. I was a literature student. When I finished my undergraduate degree, I started a master's program in English from Wichita State University, and the first year of that program I got my teaching credentials. My goal in life at that point was to be an English teacher, and I did that for about 6 months. I substitute taught in the public schools in Gillette, Wyoming.

Then, my former husband came home from work one day and said the local day care center needed a director. I knew nothing about preschool children, although I knew lots about adolescent development. I did know something about business. I had the secretarial and bookkeeping skills I had obtained to support myself through school. So I applied for the job and was hired.

So at age 24, I became the director of a county child care agency that served preschool children, most of whom were 3–5 years old. About 25% of the children had special needs of some kind, from needing a couple hours a week of speech therapy or language development to children who were very severely multiply disabled. These children were fully integrated into our program; at the time, I didn't know that there was any other way to do preschool.

The first year I spent playing catch-up in terms of my own knowledge about early childhood development and what was available. I had a sense from what I knew about how kids learn and the kind of setting I wanted to work in that I didn't like the way the preschool was structured. So I gathered up all of my teachers one day and drove over to see a Montessori preschool. I just said: "Let's go observe for a day,"and lo and behold, as we were driving back everybody said: "Gosh, we could do some of that stuff." Then we started doing a lot of reading and inservice training about individual programming for preschool kids and how one sets up such programs. We called on a couple of very good resources. For instance, there was a professor at the University of Wyoming who did several inservice training sessions with us. And a number of us were involved in starting an early childhood association, so I got training there. Also, in the summer of 1975, I talked my board into sending me to a 3-week day care management seminar. I had some very intensive day care management training at that point. So, yes, there was a lot of training along the way, but other than the day care management experience, I had no administrative training.

During that time, I had gotten very interested in family counseling. I had received a lot of inservice training in early childhood education, behavior modification, and in family counseling and dynamics and how they affect a child's life. My ex-husband and I did some co-therapy with the families at the day care center that worked out very nicely. As a result of this, I applied to a couple of graduate schools to get a master's in social work with an emphasis in family counseling. I had been accepted at the University of Kansas when I was contacted by the deputy director of Rocky Mountain Planned Parenthood in Denver. The director of development was leaving and I had been involved in starting a Planned Parenthood clinic in Gillette. He said: "You really ought to think about this job."

That was when I decided I would probably stay in human services administration. My observation at that point was that some human services agencies were managed badly and had many problems, and that people did not bring good business practices and principles to the human services field. I thought that was outrageous. Bad management caused a tremendous waste of money and people's time, and was unfair to the people who didn't get good services. So I decided if I was going to stay in human services, I would end up in administration. I was convinced I could do it better than anybody else, which sounds sort of egotistical I guess, but my administrative skills are strong, and it is something I enjoy.

I also decided at that point that if I was going to do that, I really had to have fund-raising skills. So, for 3 years at Planned Parenthood I did fund-raising. They had been willing to hire me with no fund-raising skills. That was a really good experience, plus I learned a lot from Sheri Tepper, the Executive Director at Planned Parenthood. She was a bright, innovative person and a very strong manager. We didn't always agree, but even now sometimes I'll do certain things and if I stop and think about it, I know I learned that from Sheri Tepper. The older I get, the more I understand decisions she made at the time that I didn't agree with then, but that I probably would agree with now. Plus, Planned Parenthood at that time attracted a collection of other people who had started out in a lot of other fields. We had people in business administration, we had a former nun who had been an English teacher, we had people who were in nursing and were going into administration. So I worked with this group of very bright people who were about my age, who had come from diverse backgrounds and were interested in family planning services for poor people.

Then, I answered an ad that said the Legal Center needed an executive director. That summer, 1980, I had been taking a class from Denver Free University called "Which Job is Me"? The first exercise we did in the class was to write a classified advertisement for the job that we really wanted. And, except for the fact that the ad I wrote was for a child care center, and there was a little difference in salary because we were supposed to write our ideal ad, the ad that appeared for The Legal Center position was almost word for word what I had written in class. It was unreal. It was one of those things that you look at and say: "I don't believe this"! It was the only time I had ever gotten a job for which I felt I had the skills, where someone said this is what we want you to do, and I said I can do all of those things. Up until then I had done stuff I wasn't trained to do (except for teaching).

The Legal Center serves people with disabilities who have legal problems in which the disability is central to the problem. This includes everything from employment discrimination, to Social Security eligibility, to obtaining legally mandated services. When I first started with the Legal Center, it was already the designated protection and advocacy system in Colorado for people with developmental disabilities. It has since become the designated protection and advocacy system for people with mental illnesses and the designated client assistance program for people served by our state vocational rehabilitation system.

What Are Your Likes and Dislikes about Working in Human Services? How Have These Changed over the Years, if at All?

I think what has always attracted me to this, and probably is also the reason I tried to become a teacher, was that I really felt this kind of work makes a difference in people's lives. Day care is very important to parents, and it's important that children have every edge they can possibly get before they get into school. To be involved in that, plus offer children an opportunity to go to school with other children who are different from them: that was a real plus. I didn't realize until 1975 how innovative Wyoming was in terms of its preschool services. There were 17 day training centers for preschoolers across the state. It was impressive to me that people identified a need and addressed it, and did so in a meaningful way in a state that is very sparsely populated. Certainly not every one of those 17 day training centers was in a fully integrated setting, but they all had pacesetters. There was just sort of a spirit about it, plus I loved the people that I worked with. It was fun, hard work; I felt like I was accomplishing something. We would see children come into our program with 18- to 20-month delays in terms of where they should have been chronologically, and we would see them catch up over a period of time, and know that they would be okay. That's very satisfying.

The thing that drives me crazy and makes me want to run away is when people don't take this business seriously. I think that's one of the things that makes me really sick and angry about what's happened here recently. We've lost a major program in the community because of mismanagement and irresponsibility, and that damages every single one of the people who were being served by that agency, as well as other disability programs and nonprofit organizations in the community. That's intolerable.

I came to the Legal Center from Planned Parenthood because I like being the executive director. I decided that I would rather be in this supervisory position than in a middle management position. I think people who are executive directors have a fair need for control. My protection and advocacy colleagues chuckle about that from time to time.

What has kept me at the Legal Center is a couple of things. One of them is the working relationship I have with Randy Chapman, the Director of Legal Services. We have been able to work it out so we don't get in each other's way. We really had to struggle with that a couple of times over the years. The other thing is just the nature of advocacy. The whole civil rights area becomes such a central part of your life. The problem is: What do you do after you've been a protection and advocacy director? Where do you go from here? Well, maybe one of the reasons we're building our national association, one of the things we talk and dream about, is so that we will have a national training institute for advocates where people might have an opportunity to either go into another agency for a period of time or to an institute setting for a week, and do some training and some teaching. We have a pool of incredible skill and knowledge across the country. The other thing that has kept us here, a lot of us, is the growth of the program. I think had the program been decimated, had we not had the opportunity for growth by adding the protection and advocacy system for the mentally ill and for the Client Assistance Program, a lot of us would have left because the challenge wouldn't have been as great.

The other thing that is so interesting about advocacy is that there are times when it is really very funny. The situations some people get into are outrageous. What I have noticed about very good advocates is that they have a marvelous sense of humor, and I think that is what helps us survive.

Are There Other Things that Have Changed about Why You Do What You Do? What's Good about It for You? Have the Rewards Changed?

What I see about myself is that I have become a whole lot tougher. When I was going to Wichita State University, one of my favorite books was *Teaching as a Subversive Activity*. The authors said that if you were going to be a good teacher you had to have a good "crap detector." I think that's important in whatever line of work you do, particularly in human services. People used to describe me as a very nice person, and I used to hate it. *You could go through your whole life as a nice person and not make a damned bit of difference.* I think I really like what I've learned as an advocate about being a tougher, stronger person, and not allowing people to get away with things that I would have let them get away with before. Not that I think that we go about advocacy in an aggressive or adversarial way, but we have an assertive style that we use that is very consistent in terms of how we approach problems. Internally, I find that I am not patient with a lot of things that I used to worry about. I don't tolerate some bureaucratic hassles that I would have probably let go 5 or 6 years ago when I first started in this job. I push the system in terms of my working with the people in it because I don't think we need to be pushed around. So that's something that I can feel has changed. People who have known me over a period of time have commented on that.

In terms of what else is different, I've become more cynical. It was really good for us to have a couple of college interns around this past summer, people who have a very fresh and new perspective. It was fun to be in a relationship where I had an opportunity to do some teaching with them.

Have You Found it Difficult to Balance Your Personal and Professional Lives? If So, What Works for You?

It's very difficult. It's very difficult based on the goals you set for yourself if you're a superachiever. I think that women are under a lot of pressure to do it all. In the last 3 years, I have been president of a nonprofit organization which filed under Chapter 11 bankruptcy to reorganize one of its corporations 2 years ago; I had to facilitate the board's making that decision and stay involved while they worked out of that. And I've been president of the National Association of Protection and Advocacy Systems (NAPAS). There have been times when the stress was just so incredible I wondered what in the hell I was doing. What I learned from all of that is that there probably aren't very many crises that would throw me. It would have to be just a major catastrophic event that would really undo me.

When I left the presidency of the nonprofit organization, I was literally counting the minutes. At my last board meeting, I said: "My term will be over in 18 hours, 34 minutes, and 25 seconds." The bankruptcy proceedings were the worst experience of my life. I had people yelling at me, and it was awful. I could not have done that without the support of the Legal Center board, because I was spending a lot of hours on that. Certainly, when I took that presidency I had no idea what was going to happen.

Brad (my current husband) has been enormously supportive. What we have done is we've just sort of had to work through it as its happened, and really go out of our way to plan time together. His schedule is every bit as busy as mine is. This year, I decided that I was only going to do those things that I consider fun, and that my reward for going through all of this for the last 3 years is that I'm only going to do things that will not add a significant amount of stress to my life. I'm no longer president of NAPAS—I did love that experience—and I'm going off the other board since I've been there for 8 or 9 years, and I'm starting school. I'm starting school not because I need the degree, but because I really would like to have the theory catch up with the practice. I like to learn, and when I was being recruited to enroll for this program, the administrator said that I should take at least two classes a semester or I'd never finish. I don't have to do that. If I want to take 6 years to finish this program, the catalog says I can do it. And if I only want to take one class a semester, there is nothing that precludes my doing it. I'm trying to get rid of night meetings. So I think Brad and I are both trying to figure out ways that we can spend a little more time together and have more time at home. It requires a concerted effort.

If you choose to, you can allow yourself to work all the time, and it's not healthy. I think those long, long hours and the high stress over time are why people leave the field, because they can't take it. You've got to build in some fun so you keep your perspective healthy, so you can continue to do the work that you want to. You really have to find that balance. I certainly would not want to trade my marriage for my work.

Is There Anything Else You Want to Convey to People Who Are Just Starting Out or Who Are Already in Human Services?

I would say to try to seek the balance between your work and your personal life as early as you can, because it's a good habit to get into. I think in the long run it will strengthen rather than weaken your professional opportunities.

Ask a lot of questions. Find out about the organizations you work for, how they're managed, how they're run, and understand their history. That's one of the things I've really come to understand as being very important. I don't think we as human services directors teach that enough, nor do I think people go out of their way to seek it out. How people will fit into an organization at any given time has a lot to do with the history of the organization. You can learn a lot by just taking a look at that and hearing stories of the organization. There are formal and informal histories of an organization that are important, vital, and instructive.

Learn to congratulate yourself when you've accomplished something, because in this work you may not be congratulated by others. Sometimes, you have to be satisfied with just knowing you've done a good job.

For managers, it's important to let your staff know they're part of a team and to acknowledge their achievements publicly.

Exercises

9-4. For the last time, consider the questions:
a. Can you identify with any aspect of this interview?
b. What lessons do you find in this interview that you think are important for human services professionals?

REFLECTIONS ON THE INTERVIEWS: AN OVERVIEW

Perhaps the most outstanding characteristic of all four of the human services professionals interviewed is that they all have very clear answers for themselves to the questions listed at the beginning of this chapter, and at the beginning of this book. Here, once more, are those questions with the answers we received.

What Do You Expect to Get out of Doing Human Services Work? In Other Words, What Are Your Rewards?

All four professionals are in agreement about the answer to this question: they are doing human services work because it gives them the reward of making a positive difference in people's lives. In addition, all stressed the value of their relationships with colleagues—that the people with whom they work on a daily basis are another major reason they stay in the field.

There was also considerable discussion of the limited availability of certain other rewards. Most of these professionals commented on the fact that they are not always rewarded for doing a good job. For example, Doug Bradley was specific about the salary limitations and scheduling drawbacks, and how he has found ways to work with those problems to stay in the field.

What Do You Expect to Accomplish?

None of these people expects to accomplish exactly the same thing, but all have a strong sense of what they want and can accomplish. Judith Halaszyn and Mary Anne Harvey stress systems change as one way of improving people's lives. Doug Bradley sees himself as moving eventually into a program design position to broaden his impact. Cheryl Lammers described ways to identify and achieve changes within a sometimes frustrating bureaucracy.

What Are Your Values as You Provide Services?

While we did not ask specifically about values, some of the values of each person interviewed came through in the answers. Judith Halaszyn emphasizes the value of direct-care staff and the need for an agency commitment to valuing those professionals. Doug Bradley values group therapy versus individual therapy. Cheryl Lammers stressed the need to care as much as, but no more than, the person served about the outcome of services, and to know what you can and cannot do for an individual. Mary Anne Harvey places a high value on advocacy and civil rights. Perhaps most important, these values are not just abstract ideas, but directly shape how these human services professionals act on the job.

How Should You Act While You Provide Services?

Again, we did not ask this question directly, but one answer appears in every interview. Each of these professionals discusses the importance of continued professional development, and of always learning more about how to be an effective professional.

Doug Bradley has some good advice about looking for a job that offers ways to develop professionally, and looking for a job that you can live with in terms of hours and salary. Mary Anne Harvey also has a good recommendation related to finding a job you can live with when she stresses learning the history of an organization.

One other comment about how to act comes from Mary Anne Harvey. She says: "You could go though your whole life as a nice person and not make a damned bit of difference." This is a lesson that many human services professionals, particularly women, have to learn. Sometimes the only way to translate caring into action involves being assertive and not always nice or compliant.

How Do You Manage the Stress of Working in Human Services?

The answers to this question vary, but the importance of learning effective stress management is mentioned by everyone. Specifically, all express the need to get completely away from work regularly. Also, most of them discuss the need to put work in perspective, and to remember that the whole world does not have the kinds of problems they see every day. Finally, the importance of having a good sense of humor is identified as a stress management strategy with which the authors concur wholeheartedly.

A FINAL VISIT WITH DIANA

As she finishes reading the section above, Diana says to herself: "Do I wish I'd read these interviews *before* I got into human services! I guess what I've been doing with my support group is trying to find my answers to those questions.

"Wow. A year ago, I never thought I'd last beyond a week. It's been tough, real tough at times, but I stuck with it. I don't think I'll be a probation officer all my life, but it's OK right now. Maybe I'll talk to my supervisor next week about possibly moving up.

"Oh, it's nearly time to meet the group for our first annual support celebration. Seems a far cry from a year ago."

CHOICES IN CAREER DEVELOPMENT

"What can I say? There comes a moment, as who knows
better than you, when one has to move forward, when
it is impossible to stay in the same place
without moving back."

(Cross, 1984, p. 19)

Career development can have many different meanings in human services work. Here are some of them:

1. Develop your clinical skills by enrolling in graduate school or other advanced training programs.
2. Become an administrator or manager of human services.
3. Become a teacher of human services professionals.
4. Change the types of people you serve (e.g., switch from work with abused children to work with the elderly).
5. Move into policy design or quality assurance work at a state agency.

6. Become a lobbyist for systems change within the field of human services.
7. Combine your expertise in human services with professional training in law, medicine, or business.
8. Become a consultant to service providers.
9. Engage in applied research in the human services.
10. Write about human services work.

Exercises

9-5. One way to identify your long-term professional goals is described by Dr. Dru Scott (1980, pp. 78–79). She asks you to answer the following questions:
   a. Five years from now, what do you want your work life to be like?
   b. What do you want your job title to be?
   c. Where do you want to be working?
   d. What do you want your annual salary to be?
   e. What associations do you want to belong to?
   f. What awards do you want to earn?
   In addition, we ask you to also answer these two questions:
   a. What skills do you want to have that you do not have now?
   b. What professional knowledge do you want to have that you do not have now?

Consider that careers do not move in nice straight lines: neither does a person's professional growth. What interests or motivates you now is not necessarily what will interest or motivate you 5 years from now. That is why it is helpful to ask yourself the questions above once a year. If your answers next year are different from the answers you give today, that does not mean anything is wrong. It means that your professional goals have changed, so your plans need to change to match your goals.

A FINAL WORD

If the goals of today's college students are any indication, there has been a decline in idealism in the last 25 years. There has been a large increase in the proportion of students majoring in business, as well as an increase in the number of students who expect college to lead to increased earning power.

These trends toward higher salary careers are understandable, for the $10,000 to $20,000 a year made by most human services workers is not the level of income that leads to owning a home or putting a child through college (Ehrenreich, 1986). We find these trends disturbing. Our generation came of age in the sixties, in a time when we dreamt of changing the world and making it a better, more humane place to live. We agree with Ehrenreich that:

> . . . there is something grievously wrong with a culture that values Wall Street sharks above social workers, armament manufacturers above artists, or, for that matter, corporate lawyers above homemakers. Somehow, we're going to have to make the world a little more habitable for idealists, whether they are 18 or 38.
>
> (Ehrenreich, 1986, p. 39)

This book is for the practical idealists who are trying to make the world a little more habitable for us all.

REFERENCES

Anderson, R.A. (1978). *Stress power: How to turn tension into energy.* New York: Human Services Press.

Barber, B. (1980). *Informed consent in medical therapy and research.* New Brunswick, NJ: Rutgers University Press.

Bernstein, D.A., & Borkovec, T.D. (1973). *Progressive relaxation training: A manual for the helping professions.* Champaign, IL: Research Press.

Bernstein, G.S., Ziarnik, J.P., Rudrud, E.H., & Czajkowski, L.A. (1981). *Behavioral habilitation through proactive programming.* Baltimore: Paul H. Brookes Publishing Co.

Bracken, P. (1969, December). Peg Bracken's 108 original sins. *McCall's,* pp. 74–75, 138.

Bramson, R.M. (1981). *Coping with difficult people.* New York: Ballantine Books.

Brody, J. (1985). *Jane Brody's good food book.* New York: Norton.

Burgess, R.L., & Richardson, R.A. (1984). Coercive interpersonal contingencies as a determinant of child maltreatment: Implications for treatment and prevention. In R.F. Dangel & R.A. Polster (Eds.), *Parent training* (pp. 239–259). New York: Guilford.

Corey, G., Corey, M.S., & Callanan, P. (1988). *Issues and ethics in the helping professions.* Pacific Grove, CA: Brooks/Cole.

Cross, A. (1984). *Sweet death, kind death.* New York: E.P. Dutton.

Duncan, P.K., & Lloyd, K.E. (1982). Training format in industrial behavior modification. In R.M. O'Brien, A.M. Dickinson, & M.P. Rosow (Eds.), *Industrial behavior modification* (pp. 387–404). New York: Pergamon.

D'Zurilla, T.J. (1987). Problem-solving therapies. In K.S. Dobson (Ed.), *Handbook of cognitive-behavior therapy.* New York: Guilford Press.

Ehrenreich, B. (1986, October). Premature pragmatism. *Ms. Magazine,* pp. 38–39.

Ellis, A., & Harper, R.A. (1976). *A new guide to rational living.* North Hollywood, CA: Wilshire.

Fadiman, C. (1985). *The Little, Brown book of anecdotes.* Boston: Little, Brown.

Fisher, R., & Ury, W. (1981). *Getting to yes.* New York: Penguin.

Fleming, D.C., Fleming, E.R., Roach, K.S., & Oksman, P.F. (1985). Conflict management. In C.A. Maher (Ed.), *Professional self-management: Techniques for special services providers* (pp. 65–84). Baltimore: Paul H. Brookes Publishing Co.

Forman, S.G., & Cecil, M.A. (1985). Stress management. In C.A. Maher (Ed.), *Professional self-management: Techniques for special services providers* (pp. 45–63). Baltimore: Paul H. Brookes Publishing Co.

Gardner, J.F. & Chapman, M.S. (1985). *Staff development in mental retardation services: A practical handbook*. Baltimore: Paul H. Brookes Publishing Co.

Gaylin, W. (1981). In the beginning: Helpless and dependent. In W. Gaylin, I. Glasser, S. Marcus, & D.J. Rothman (Eds.), *Doing good: The limits of benevolence* (pp. 1–38). New York: Pantheon Books.

Gendler, J.R. (1984). *The book of qualities*. Berkeley: Turquoise Mountain Publications.

Giampa, F.L., Walker-Burt, G., & Lamb, D. (Eds.). (1984). *Michigan Department of Mental Health Community Direct Care Staff Curriculum*. Lansing: Office of Resource Development.

Gilbert, T.F. (1978). *Human competence: Engineering worthy performance*. New York: McGraw-Hill.

Glasser, I. (1981). Prisoners of benevolence: Power versus liberty in the welfare state. In W. Gaylin, I. Glasser, S. Marcus & D.J. Rothman (Eds.), *Doing good: The limits of benevolence* (pp. 97–170). New York: Pantheon Books.

Goodman, E.G. (1981). *At large*. New York: Summit Books.

Goodman, E.G. (1985). *Keeping in touch*. New York: Summit Books.

Greenberg, S.F. (1984). *Stress and the teaching profession*. Baltimore: Paul H. Brookes Publishing Co.

Greenberg, S.F., & Valletutti, P.J. (1980). *Stress and the helping professions*. Baltimore: Paul H. Brookes Publishing Co.

Hauck, P.A. (1967). *The rational management of children*. New York: Libra.

Hayakawa, S.I. (1964). *Language in thought and action*. New York: Harcourt, Brace, & World.

Heinlein, R.A. (1968). *The moon is a harsh mistress*. New York: Berkeley.

Holmes, T.H., & Rahe, R.H. (1967). The Social Readjustment Rating Scale. *Journal of Psychosomatic Research, 11,* 213–218.

Jaffe, D.T., & Scott, C.D. (1984). *From burnout to balance*. New York: McGraw-Hill.

Kirsta, A. (1986). *The book of stress survival*. New York: Simon & Schuster.

Kruzas, A.T. (1982). *Social service organizations and agencies directory*. Detroit: Gale Research Co.

Lovaas, I.O. (1987). Behavioral treatment and normal educational and intellectual functioning in young autistic children. *Journal of Consulting and Clinical Psychology, 55,* 3–9.

Maher, C.A., & Cook, S.A. (1985). Time management. In C.A. Maher (Ed.), *Professional self-management: Techniques for special services providers* (pp. 23–43). Baltimore: Paul H. Brookes Publishing Co.

Mallon, T. (1984). *A book of one's own: People and their diaries*. New York: Ticknor & Fields.

Martin, J. (1982). *Miss manners' guide to excruciatingly correct behavior*. New York: Atheneum.

Martin, J. (1985). *Common courtesy: In which Miss Manners solves the problem that baffled Mr. Jefferson*. New York: Atheneum.

McInerney, J.F. (1985). Authority management. In C.A. Maher (Ed.), *Professional self-management: Techniques for special services providers* (pp. 129–148). Baltimore: Paul H. Brookes Publishing Co.

McMullin, R.C. (1987). *Talk sense to yourself: A guide to cognitive restructuring therapies*. New York: Institute for Rational Emotive Psychotherapy.

Medved, R.M., & Burns, J.P. (1983). *Staff development.* Albany: Office of Mental Retardation and Developmental Disabilities.

Murphy, D.J. (1987). How to get along with the boss. *Practical Supervision,* No. 63, 1–3.

Neuhauser, D. (1982). The really effective health care service delivery system. In S. Spirn & D.W. Benfer, (Eds.), *Issues in health care management* (pp. 153–160). Rockville, MD: Aspen Systems.

Nicoloff, L.K. (1985). *Changing campus environments to support the lesbian/gay experience.* Paper presented at the Third Annual Campus Ecology Symposium, Pingree Park, Colorado.

Practical Supervision. (1986). Review of *Just in time. Practical Supervision, No. 52,* 5.

Pryor, K. (1984). *Don't shoot the dog.* New York: Bantam Books.

Romanczyk, R.G., & Kistner, J.A. (1982). Psychosis and mental retardation: Issues of coexistence. In J.L. Matson & R.P. Barrett (Eds.), *Psychopathology in the mentally retarded* (pp. 147–194). New York: Grune & Stratton.

Rosoff, A.J. (1981). *Informed consent: A guide for the health care professions.* Rockville, MD: Aspen Systems.

Rothman, D.J. (1981). The state as parent: Social policy in the progressive era. In W. Gaylin, I. Glasser, S. Marcus & D.J. Rothman (Eds.), *Doing good: The limits of benevolence* (pp. 67–96). New York: Pantheon Books.

Russ, J. (1983). *How to suppress women's writing.* Austin: University of Texas Press.

Sagan, C. (1977). *The dragons of Eden.* New York: Ballantine Books.

Scott, D. (1980). *How to put more time in your life.* New York: Signet.

Selye, H. (1976). *The stress of life.* New York: McGraw-Hill.

Sorrels, R. (Performer). (1985). *Live . . . Then came the children* (Recording). Vancouver: Aural Tradition Records.

Turnbull, H.R. III, (Ed.). (1977). *Consent handbook.* American Association on Mental Deficiency Special Publication #3.

Vash, C.L. (1984). Evaluation from the client's point of view. In A.S. Halpern & M.J. Fuhrer (Eds.), *Functional assessment in rehabilitation* (pp. 253–267). Baltimore: Paul H. Brookes Publishing Co.

Warschaw, T.A. (1980). *Winning by negotiation.* New York: McGraw-Hill.

Webster's New World Dictionary. (1962). Cleveland: The World Publishing Co.

Weldon, F. (1984). *Letters to Alice on first reading Jane Austen.* New York: Taplinger Publishing.

Woody, R.H. (1984). *The law and the practice of human services.* San Francisco: Jossey-Bass.

Ziarnik, J.P. (1980). Developing proactive direct care staff. *Mental Retardation, 18*(6), 289–292.

Zins, J.E. (1985). Work relations management. In C.A. Maher (Ed.), *Professional self-management: Techniques for special services providers* (pp. 105–127). Baltimore: Paul H. Brookes Publishing Co.

USEFUL RESOURCES

Bolles, R.N. (1986). *What color is your parachute?* Berkeley: Ten Speed Press.

Bramson, R.M. (1981). *Coping with difficult people.* New York: Ballantine Books.

Curtis, J.D., & Deteint, R.A. (1981). *How to relax.* Palo Alto: Mayfield.

Davis, M., Eshelman, E.R., & McKay, M. (1982). *The relaxation and stress reduction workbook.* Oakland: New Harbinger Publishers.

Kriegel, R., & Harris Kriegel, M. (1984). *The C zone: Peak performance under pressure.* New York: Fawcett Columbia.

Lorwen, L. (1983). *How to find and land your first full-time job.* New York: Arco.

Rogers, E.J. (1982). *Getting hired.* Englewood Cliffs, NJ: Prentice-Hall.

Scott, D. (1980). *How to put more time in your life.* New York: Charles Scribner's Sons.

Warschaw, T.A. (1980). *Winning by negotiation.* New York: McGraw-Hill.

Index